SLA GUIDELINES

Voice and Vision

Essential Issues around Diversity and Inclusion for School Libraries

Jake Hope

Series Editor: Geoff Dubber

Acknowledgements

With grateful thanks to Chris Moore and Anne Fine without whose support this publication would not have been possible. Thanks too to the many authors, illustrators, publishers, librarians and bloggers who have discussed and shared their views and thoughts with me around diversity. It feels important that consideration of this key area is an ongoing discourse and a conversation that embraces all views and opinions so as to be representative. Although it has not been possible to include all areas of debate held during the writing of this, these thoughts have nonetheless been hugely fruitful in formulating ideas and format.

Sincere thanks also to the contributors who expressed their thoughts and opinions for this publication:
Andrew Beasley, Pamela Berry, Malorie Blackman, Anne Fine, Cordelia Fine, Giancarlo Gemin, Debi Gliori, Katrina Gutierrez, Will Hill, Catherine Johnson, Patrice Lawrence, Amy McKay, Glenda Millard, Chris Moore, Ifeoma Onyefulu, Alex Strick, Steve Tasane, Alex Wheatle.

The SLA Publications Team would like to thank SLA Board colleagues Margaret Pemberton and Rosalind Buckland for their useful comments on the draft text.

Published by
School Library Association
1 Pine Court, Kembrey Park
Swindon SN2 8AD

Tel: 01793 530166   Fax: 01793 481182
E-mail: info@sla.org.uk
Web: www.sla.org.uk

Registered Charity No: 313660
Charity Registered in Scotland No: SC039453

Cover: Kerri-Jo Stewart from Vancouver, Canada (https://commons.wikimedia.org/wiki/File:Independence_Day_Parade_-_Flickr_-_Kerri-Jo_(275).jpg), "Independence Day Parade - Flickr - Kerri-Jo (275)", https://creativecommons.org/licenses/by/2.0/legalcode

Printed by Holywell Press, Oxford

Contents

Introduction

A definition of Diversity taken from the *Cambridge English Dictionary*.

> *The fact of many different types of things or people being included in something; a range of different things or people... The fact that there are many different ideas and opinions about something.*

— http://dictionary.cambridge.org/dictionary/english/diversity (accessed 6.6.17)

The world that children and young people are growing up in is one where they increasingly encounter and experience people from different backgrounds and who have needs that might vary from their own. The fashions and fabrics people are clothed in, the music they listen to, the television and content they watch, even the language used to connect and communicate with others is increasingly influenced by an ever broadening range of cultural influences.

We all have different make-ups, and these produce altered personal perspectives on the world. Sometimes those can sit together easily, at other points there can be tensions or difficulties that arise. As communication technologies develop and as people travel and migrate more, there becomes an increasing need to broach some of these issues of difference and the reasons for them and to raise awareness and understanding in order that our similarities and synergies rather than our difference and perhaps difficulties caused by those can be identified and appreciated.

We are all very conscious that as a society, we need to understand the needs of others more fully, to better realise our own place and position in the world and theirs and to recognise the wealth of ways there are of leading our lives and reaching the goals and milestones involved with these.

Discussion of diversity can become highly charged – this issue can have the danger of being presented as a series of thorny issues within a set of highly politicised agendas. We are in danger of having our comments and decisions criticised and labelled as sexist, homophobic or racist. There's a real need to move beyond this name-calling and move into a deeper exploration of the provision of diversity itself and the range of issues that have arisen and continue to manifest themselves.

The words and pictures that young people encounter at the early stages of growing up, when our personality and identity are malleable and plastic, have the real ability to contribute towards their sense of identity and self-image. The world of children's literature can be limitless and without boundaries, showing true diversity across the globe. Effective school libraries and learning resource centres fulfil a vital role as the heart and lungs of a school, producing the essential oxygen of knowledge and learning whilst providing an essential context for an individual's self-led learning and also a support for the more formal education offer made by the institution itself. Highlighting and celebrating the diversity of humankind, both in terms of the library's resource collection and the activities and promotions it engages with, is a way of offering an understanding of the nature of diversity and will present opportunities to consider those complementary differences and tensions for all students across the school regardless of their age, ethnicity, background and make-up.

Section 1: What is Diversity?

An Umbrella Term

Diversity is an umbrella term that embraces a wide range of component parts. These can include, but are not limited to:

- Class
- Sexuality
- Mental health
- Race
- Religion
- Physical make-up.

Some individuals and groups object to the term 'Diversity', feeling that it is too broad and amorphous to allow meaningful application. It is precisely this breadth, however, that enables us to recognise some of the challenges and changes we need to understand in terms of the literature that is published, presented and promoted. With the finite number of titles that any school library is able to buy and for which it can provide shelf-space, it feels appropriate to consider the overall representation of diversity that we can create and to carefully consider some of the over-arching issues and themes. In so doing it is important not to diminish or exclude voices, but rather to construct the most accurate picture of human activity that we can.

The Case for Embracing – a Diverse Approach

For some, the term diversity might appear distant and irrelevant to them, one that impacts or affects only others. Diversity affects all of us however, and to be meaningful it has to embrace all of us. Some aspects of diversity will necessarily relate to us in direct ways, whilst others only indirectly. It can be challenging. It can put a spotlight on to some of the assumptions we hold, whether consciously or more implicitly and it can demonstrate some of the patterns of our thinking and actions. Sometimes this might make us feel uncomfortable. It might also induce a reluctance to engage in discussion for fear of getting things wrong or causing offence. In a school library context it is useful to recognise that a proactive and sensitive approach to the subject – its provision and promotion – will always be better than an avoidance of the issue and a denial of discussion on this important subject.

Diversity as a Component of Identity

A sense of personal identity is built up from many interlocking components; from our background experiences, our thoughts and our bodies. These influences act as broad brushstrokes to illustrate us – who we are and how we feel; helping us to bring together aspects and chapters of our own lives for ourselves and for others. It is important to note, however, that as much as there can be similarities in background and experience between many of us, there can also be vast differences in how these are viewed by others and the level of significance or importance that is attributed to them. It is equally important to avoid making assumptions or judgements about children and young people based upon one specific element of their identity. Teenage maturation during the ages 11 and 18 can be a time of great change and exploration and as we all know whilst that can be personally invigorating, it can also feel disorientating. Huge change is taking place in both the brain and body. Having access to a range of library materials that offer insight into differing and different ways of life and differing aspirations can be a way to provide context both for those young people that find themselves directly affected. Whilst some aspects of the term 'Diversity' might feel complex and sophisticated, they are also massively exciting and affect the core of who we are!

Diversity and the World of Publications

Diversity within publications can be broken down into two types.

1 The first of these provide their audience with an insight into a particular culture or group, helping to highlight some of the key aspects that make up this lifestyle. Writing of this genre will contribute to the reader's greater understanding and empathy with this culture or group. This type of writing can usefully be termed 'windows into worlds' and whilst it offers a viewing point into a different individual or community's lifestyles, in and of themselves it is *not* diverse as it represents only the single view of the author. This is not to say there is no value to works of this type. They offer a depth of field that allows greater understanding and, arguably, is more likely to achieve attitudinal change through raising awareness. Although not diverse of themselves, these publications as part of a library's collection, play a valuable and vital role in ensuring that collections as a whole are diverse.

2 The other type of diverse publication or content brings together a range of different lifestyles and individuals in one title. These are diverse in and of themselves and can highlight some of the differences – and indeed similarities – between lifestyles and experiences. These are less likely to explore diversity to the same depth, due to the need to balance out each element.

These different sorts of publication are important to recognise when collection development is being considered and management strategies are being created.

Pathway from the Past towards Change

Publishing for children and young people has traditionally reflected a somewhat narrow demographic. There are many reasons why this is the case. It's not helpful to criticise any individuals, groups or organisations, but to explore some of the rationale and in so doing, to hopefully identify pathways to change.

Embracing diversity in a collection of library resources can be challenging. There is not always a culture or precedent for writing among some of our diverse communities, or if there is, it may be that the writers are not always aware of the formal process through which manuscripts are considered for publication.

Publishers of titles for children and young people need to balance commercial viability with educational and social need. This is not always an easy line to tread. We need to consider the people employed in publishing itself. Even at the level of regional rep. positions in publishing companies, Children's & Young People's posts have not often been filled by a diverse work force. In order to see a wider selection pool for publishing staff it may be necessary to remove a degree-level education as an essential criteria on a person spec. There is also a challenge in selection of material for publication. Management decisions made to commission and support titles that are diverse may unwittingly be overlooked due to editors' lack of knowledge or understanding about particular ethnic, religious, social or other groups. In targeting those specific groups themselves to buy publications some do not have a culture of visiting bookshops or libraries that means we need to try different approaches to reaching these audiences.

Libraries and booksellers do not always stock a range of titles that reflect our increasingly diverse 21st century society.

- This may be because books on these issues are not seen as useful additions to the lists or perhaps some specific minority groups are not championed at times when most money is being spent.
- It may be that in the opinion of the buyer the targeted readers are not 'diverse' and perhaps there is no ready market for or interest in these titles.
- It may be that there simply is not enough knowledge of the range and depth of titles that are being published or an understanding of ways to promote them.

Whatever the reasons that lie behind the often narrow range of stock held by many booksellers and that sit on library shelves, the outcome is often that titles that reflect diversity is its various guises are often not seen by a readership that would often be willing and interested to broaden their knowledge of the work, thoughts and actions of other groups other than themselves.

Individuals might not be in the habit of reading diverse titles. We all know it can be difficult to wean young teenagers, some who are undoubtedly enthusiastic readers, from a particular author or series. Of course it may be for cultural reasons – readers or their parents/guardians might have concerns or fears that reading about a different group or value system might present a challenge to their own cultural or their family's established system of beliefs. This could be overt or covert censorship. There may be practical reasons too – some groups do not have a culture of reading. This can lead to a devaluing of books, libraries and resources at home with an inevitable narrowing of ideas. It may simply be that the young person whatever their culture, creed, ethnic or religious group feels that the books they see at school do not reflect their own lives and so feels a lack of engagement or a sense of disenfranchisement. They therefore never seem able to develop an empathy for other people who live, act and work in different ways from their own.

The net result can be to create a vicious circle in which existing attitudes, beliefs and behaviours are perpetuated even though the world around us is rapidly changing. To bring about change in the thoughts and actions of children and young people – to encourage and persuade them to empathise with others and appreciate differences and similarities and respect the needs and beliefs of others the publishing world and school librarians need to take on a radical and holistic approach to the subject of diversity. In our busy, hectic world this is challenging.

A Guide to Types of Diversity in Books

There are many facets to diversity – we need to remember that different sets of people and some wider communities are under-represented in our schools and more broadly in our UK society. They have specific or specialised needs which are often ignored. Identifying and then satisfying the needs of these groups can sometimes feel a little overwhelming for us all, complicated further by our concerns and confusions as terminology changes, so too acceptable points of view. We are all aware of 'political correctness' when discussing these issues. This can mean that many of us in society at large worry about the ways we discuss and approach these challenges and the fact that we may get it wrong.

The following booklist offers a simple insight into some of the key issues of diversity. It also goes some way to explain useful terminology. Let's all remember that culture is always on the move – it does not stand still, and so that as the world changes then the types of language or lexicon that we use also shifts and changes too, as does our understanding of all aspects and shades of the human condition.

Social Class

As a general rule characters and themes in children's books have predominantly focused on the middle or upper classes. Although exceptions to this can be found through the history and development of children's literature – Charles Kingsley's *The Water Babies*, Frances Hodgson Burnett's *The Prince and the Pauper* and even Enid Blyton's *Six Bad Boys* – these tend to serve a narrative function or are used as a politicised social lever – rather than being truly representative. Kimberley Reynolds suggests in *Left Out: The Forgotten Tradition of Radical Publishing for Children in Britain 1910–1949*[1] that the ideals of healthy, well-nourished middle class children as protagonists in children's literature become a 'model or measure' and that the exclusion of the poor or their negative depiction establishes them as being dysgenic (Reynolds, *Left Out*, 2016, OUP), or having a negative genetic impact.

Eve Garnett's book, *The Family from One End Street* was hailed upon its publication as one of the first novels for children to represent a working class family as its protagonists. It was awarded the Carnegie Medal in 1938 and has endured, although some of its depictions of education – particularly in terms of literacy and mathematics are not always enlightened.

Reflections of class are more likely to be found with notable authors like Frank Cottrell Boyce, Elen Caldecott, Cathy Cassidy, Siobhan Curham, Phil Earle, Polly Ho-Yen, Anthony McGowan, Robert Swindells, Robert Westall and Jacqueline Wilson. It remains true that many of the aspirations and attitudes of literature for children and young adults are often consistently middle class in formulation and expression.

In the book *Children's Reading Choices*, Hall and Coles[2] state that 'socio-economic circumstances and family background are highly significant factors in children's reading choices and habits.' Commenting on this Ludvigsen cites that 'children in social class A on average read

---

[1] Reynolds, Kimberley, (2016), *Left Out: The Forgotten Tradition of Radical Publishing for Children in Britain 1910–1949*. Oxford University Press

[2] Hall C and Coles M, (1999), *Children's Reading Choices*. Routledge

2.92 books and children growing up in D/E families only read 2.4 books in the previous month'. While Ludvigsen[3] cautions about findings that ignore the children from lower income backgrounds who do read books, there is an argument to suggest that if more books reflected their lifestyles and backgrounds it might provide a greater incentive for these children to read more widely and frequently.

What to look for in books

- Consider the characters and their presentation
- How is their home life presented?
- Are there elements of condescension – albeit unwitting – in terms of how characters develop and the situations they face?
- Is class depicted as an obstacle to be overcome in order to attain towards a middle class set of values?

Further reading for those interested in finding out more can be found in:

Bennett, T. M. Savage, E. Silva, M. Gayo-Cal and D. Wright (2009) *Culture, Class, Distinction*, Routledge.

Hall, C. and Coles, M (1999), *Children's Reading Choices*, Routledge.

Reynold, Kimberley, *Left Out*.

Physical Make-Up

Many children's books feature a very idealised portrayal of childhood – which it patently isn't for most children – a Romantic ideal, a continuation of thinking from the Romantic period with ideas of and actions that show main characters with an innate sense of goodness and morality who reflect this both in terms of their mental and cognitive behaviours and also in terms of bodily representation.

Where early examples of physical diversity are seen, this is often to emphasise the overcoming of a personal struggle, signifying types of resilience and personal progress that might just as readily be manifested externally as internally – Colin in *The Secret Garden* is able to overcome his illness through time outdoors and the good-hearted nurturing that Mary Lennox and Dickon offer to him. Likewise, Clara in Johann Spyri's *Heidi* is able to cast aside her wheelchair due to the nurture of Heidi and her grandfather and the restorative qualities of the Alpine mountain air and lifestyle.

If only life was really like that!

More recently titles have tended to take a step towards a more realistic depiction, exploring and highlighting how everyday life can be for many, the impact of change and crises on people's lives and some of the ups as well as the downs associated with different conditions and body issues. Authors to look out for include Rachel Anderson, Andrew Beasley, Sarah Crossan, Susie Day, Joyce Dunbar, Michael Foreman, Patrick Ness, Sophie Smiley, Jeanne Willis and Jacqueline Wilson.

---

[3] Ludvigsen, Anna, (2014) 'Bookshelfie: Book Ownership, Class and Families'
http://discoversociety.org/2014/01/06/bookshelfie-book-ownership-class-and-families/

The 'Special Educational Needs and Disability Act' (2001),[4] outlines the *'duty to educate children with special educational needs in mainstream schools.'* (Section 316). The Equality Act 2010,[5] states that schools must not discriminate against pupils because of their disability. Part of this includes making reasonable adjustments to remove barriers that might face these pupils. This includes ensuring access to help and support within the school and to learning activities and materials. This has consequences in our own area of responsibility – for the School Library, its physical make-up and layout.

Adjustments can be made to provision through consideration of access and space within the library itself, the height of shelving, work units, computers and static digital devices. A range of large print books and audiobooks can also help ensure greater accessibility for our children and young people with visual impairments. Barrington Stoke www.barringtonstoke.co.uk produce books that are 'super readable' and that have production values – typography, size, spacing and paper choices – which have been selected to ensure ease of access for those with reading difficulties, including dyslexia and visual impairment. Barrington Stoke have also created an app., 'Tints' which enables options for the selection of a page background colour and for a reading ruler. A variety of gels and magnifiers are also available as support.

The RNIB www.rnib.org.uk and Calibre www.calibre.org.uk/ are able to provide a range of practical support to readers with visual impairments. Do contact them to discover what they have to offer.

Remember too your local public lending librarians – they may well offer you useful advice/support and also make available their supply of e-audiobooks for your users.

The National Deaf Society www.ndcs.org.uk/ will also be pleased to offer guidance and support for students with hearing difficulties and ensuring access.

Scope ran a project in collaboration with children's book charity Booktrust, called In the Picture.[6] The campaign had the following mission statement:

> *Scope's In the Picture campaign raises awareness of the need to include disabled children in the books they read.*

Further information about the initiative can be found on the Scope website which also includes Scope publications, free storybooks available in PDF format and colouring sheets and activities (http://www.scope.org.uk/support/families/books/children).

What to look for in books

Where books are illustrated,

- Are characters shown with any supportive devices like glasses, hearing aids, wheelchairs or sticks?

- Are there sensitivities in terms of the different groups? For example there can sometimes be divides between lip reading and sign language in deaf communities.

- Is there a balance between realism and empowerment? In some books magic is used to

---

[4] Special Educational Needs and Disability Act (2001) http://www.legislation.gov.uk/ukpga/2001/10/section/1

[5] The Equality Act (2010) http://www.legislation.gov.uk/ukpga/2010/15/contents

[6] In the Picture https://www.scope.org.uk/support/families/books/children

overcome physical struggles but for children whose condition is unlikely to improve or is even degenerative, this might be profoundly demoralising.

Further reading for those interested in finding out more can be found in:

Prater, Mary Anne. Dyches, Tina (2008). *Teaching about disabilities through children's literature,* Libraries Unlimited.

Sexuality

We all know that children and young people's sense of sexual identity slowly emerges, increasing in speed with the onset of hormonal change in the early teenage years. Personal feelings, doubts, urges and impulses can be confusing, contradictory and challenging; sometimes almost overwhelmingly so. The onset of this period of adolescence is often fraught with difficulty for young people and those around them. Books on the subject of sexuality can often provide a useful personal yardstick to measure one's own physical growth, development and emotional and sexual urges. They need to be freely available on your library shelves, so too information from a range of organisations that deal with all teenage issues where they can be browsed, borrowed and read in private.

Heteronormative

Titles exploring sexuality are often heteronormative and promote the idea of heterosexuality, or being straight, as the mainstream. Relationships between one man and one woman are seen as the normal or default sexual orientation from which other approaches therefore deviate. This approach was advocated through the Schools Curriculum where the recommendation was made that only heterosexual intercourse should be explained and explored in classroom teaching, thereby creating an assumption that heterosexuality is the 'norm'. (Epstein, Debbie (1993).)[7] Despite the increased focus on this construction of sexuality, there are still myriad approaches and subjects explored through this.

In the history of children's literature, it has often proved the case that relationships ended with marriage before they were consummated. For a long period, sexualised behaviour was seen as abhorrent, the mildly seductive flirtation that occurs in Coolidge's *What Katy Did at School* is viewed with contempt and likewise in C. S. Lewis' *The Last Battle*, Susan Pevensie is no longer a friend of Narnia and has stopped believing due to favouring nylons, lipsticks and invitations, the moment she becomes sexualised. As Jill states, 'She always was a jolly sight too keen on being grown-up'.[8]

The first real exploration of sexual development and relationships occurred with the growth of Young Adult fiction in the United States and arose with titles like Judy Blume's *Forever*. The book explores a first sexual relationship between Katherine Danziger and Michael Wagner and indications are implied that their friend Artie might be gay. The book was ground-breaking due to its frank, unsentimental portrayal of sexuality, but has however proved controversial and has been banned by some education authorities and libraries in different parts of the world for this very reason. In the United Kingdom Alan Garner's *Red Shift* explores fear associated with sex. Throughout the course of Aidan Chamber's *Dance Sequence*, a collection of six novels that experiment with language and form, sexuality and its emergence is a central premise of young adult identity. As Young Adult literature has developed and grown, there have been more explorations of sexual identity. Even in those which might be termed heteronormative, there is a wealth of approaches and attitudes available including those which are focused of developing relationships of varying intensity, looking at consequences of pregnancy, exploring abuse and even incest.

---

[7] Epstein, Debbie, (1993), 'Practising Heterosexuality,' *Curriculum Studies*, 1:2, 275-286

[8] Lewis, C. S. (1956), *The Last Battle*. The Bodley Head

Sexual relationships are explored for younger readers in a number of factual titles that explore reproduction as part of science and the human body. There are also titles like Morris Gleitzman's *Adult's Only* which explore sexual education and parental sex and Babette Coles' humorous *When Mummy Laid an Egg*.

Homosexuality

Homosexuality, or gay and lesbian sex, has slowly and hesitantly entered books for children and young people. Early portrayals of this in literature for young people include Jean Ure's *The Other Side of the Fence* (published in 1986) which explores a rift between Richard and his father following his coming out and places this alongside the heterosexual Bonny. Aidan Chambers' *Dance on My Grave* explores the relationship between Henry and Barry, as is typical with Chamber's Dance sequence of novels, it is told in a variety of constructed media and uses verbal play.

The reflection of homosexuality in literature for children and young adults was hindered by Section 28 of the Local Government Act 1988. This stated that local authorities *'shall not intentionally promote homosexuality [or] promote the teaching in any maintained school of the acceptability of homosexuality as a pretended family relationship'*.[9] This had a limiting effect upon the types of literature available through school libraries and thereby constrained the market for publishers.

Writers like David Levithan, Julie Burchill and Juno Dawson (formerly writing under James Dawson) have added appreciably to the body of work available. Dawson is particularly notable for having written *This Book is Gay*, which explores gender and sexuality for young people looking at issues around family and friends and playing a valuable role in normalising experiences, its style is informal and easy to dip into.

Books for younger readers exploring homosexuality often focus around families and same sex parenting and include titles like Justin Richardson's *And Tango Makes Three* and Morris Gleitzman's *Two Weeks with the Queen*.

Bisexuality

This is where an individual is attracted to and may have sexual relationships with people of male and female genders. Statutory curriculum requirements about sex education and Section 28 similarly stymied development in this area. Even now there is little mainstream representation – check out Sarra Manning's *Pretty Things*, Lil Wilkinson's *Pink* and Cassandra Clare's *Shadowhunters* which all feature bisexuality.

Polyamorous

Polyamorous relationships are those where relationships are held with more than one partner with the knowledge and consent of all partners. There is debate as to whether polyamory is an approach to the holding of relationships, or whether it should be deemed a sexual orientation or identity in its own right. Polyamorous relationships are often diverse in and of themselves depending upon the individuals within them. At the time of writing there has been little coverage or exploration of polyamorous relationships within fiction for children and young adults

---

[9] Local Government Act (1988), section 28 http://www.legislation.gov.uk/ukpga [26/12/2016]

in the United Kingdom, Alex Sanchez's *Boyfriends with Girlfriends* and his *Rainbow* book series come to mind as partly exploring this. There have been movements across social media platforms advocating this development in children's writing

Asexuality

Asexuality is a lack of sexual attraction to anyone regardless of gender and a low or non-existent desire and libido for sexual activity. A study conducted in 2004 identified 1% of the British population as being asexual. Bogaert, Anthony F. (2004) 'Asexuality: prevalence and associated factors in a national probability sample' *Journal of Sex Research*. 41 (3): 279-87. As with polyamorous relationships, at the time of writing there has been little coverage or exploration of asexuality within fiction for children and young adult in the United Kingdom, although Alex Sachez's 'Rainbow' books do feature this. Again there have been movements across social media which have called for this to be reflected in writing for young people

Key authors to look out for when exploring issues of sexuality include Aidan Chambers, Julie Burchill, Juno Dawson, Liz Kessler, David Levithan, Patrick Ness, Paul Magrs, Tabitha Suzuma, Alex Sanchez.

What to look for in books

- Do books refer to sexuality in a way that assumes or implies that a particular sexuality is a default position?
- Are a range of characters portrayed and shown with different sexual interests and urges?
- Are the sexual relationships, urges and interests that are depicted within books questioned and explored?
- Do they ever feel tokenistic and are characters always rounded and convincing?

Further reading for those interested in finding out more can be found in:

Epstein, B. (2013) *'Are the kids all right?': Representations of LGBTQ characters in children's and young adult literature*, Hammeron Press.

James, Kathryn, (2011), *Death, gender and sexuality in contemporary adolescent literature*, Routledge.

Pugh, Tison, (2014), *Innocence, Hereosexuality, and the Queerness of Children's Literature*, Routledge.

Gender

Biologically, gender in us is determined by our possession of specific reproductive organs and the associated secondary sexual characteristics resulting from these and our hormone production. Culturally, however, there are many attributes, responses in behaviour, roles and even the type of responses and expectations held in education that are often considered or constructed as distinct differences between males and females. Books for children and young people have sometimes perpetuated somewhat rigid ideas about female and male roles and cultural expectations; for young readers the concern is that these images translate into the types of aspirations they might hold. Stereotype might easily be conveyed through illustrations or written text.

Lauren Child, the 10th Waterstone's Children's Laureate, stated on her appointment in June 2017:

> Boys don't like reading books that have girls as the main characters – and that 'makes it harder for girls to be equal'.

Stereotyping

Discussion has long been held on supposed differences in gender and whether these are natural and hard-wired or the result of social conditioning. Titles that are gender specific such as *The Big Beautiful Colouring Book for Girls* or *The Big Brilliant Colour Book for Boys* can be limiting and reductive in terms of overall readership but also in terms of aspiration and interest appeal. This became the focus of a social media campaign, *Let Books Be Books*[10] attracting considerable interest and so convincing that publishers Usborne, Buster Books and others have discontinued publication of gender specific titles.

Books and content have the ability to shine a light upon aspects of society and long-held or deep-rooted assumptions. Illustrations can provide powerful mental images. It is often the case that the visual portrayal of females in a very restrictive way; girls in frilly dresses and with immaculately coiffured hair, are unlikely to be able to engage in types of boisterous activity or adventure. Their apparel instead makes them objects of aesthetic beauty. Some classic picture books that we present to children time and again contain secondary characters in very outdated roles with women shown as cooking, cleaning and looking after children and dads shown working or returning from work. The value of the titles themselves and the contributions they make to a collection needs consideration, but how to balance out such issues within the collection needs to be thought through, as too does the appropriateness of selecting these for any shared reading promotions like storytimes or reading clubs.

Tomboy George, in Enid Blyton's *The Famous Five*, challenges many gender stereotypes, unlike Anne in the same series, she subverts expectations and pushes the boundaries of what her two male cousins, Julian and Dick expect of her. Gene Kemp's Carnegie winning novel, *The Turbulent Term of Tyke Tyler* cleverly disrupts reader expectations of her protagonist and together with Anne Fine's *Bill's New Frock* which lithely avoids gender specificity and allow readers an insight into some of the unsaid and all-too-often unchallenged expectations and attitudes around gender and behaviour.

---

10 Loughrey, Clarisse (29 January, 2016), 'Publisher to Drop Gendered Children's Titles after 'Let Books be Books' campaign,' Independent

Feminism

A movement against narrow and clichéd approaches to gender constructions has been gaining popularity with authors and publishers making attempts to explore feminist approaches as portrayed and exhibited through literature and through this the promotion of equality of rights and opportunities. A key area for consideration here is the increased prominence and coverage given to the many female innovators in the fields of both science and arts, thereby showcasing their important societal contributions and helping to raising female aspirations in these important fields of science, culture and social improvement.

Boys' Literacy

Conversely, picture book author Jonathan Emmett believes there is also a gender bias in picture books that means boys' tastes are under-represented due to the lack of male gate-keepers working in the children's book sector. His *'Cool Not Cute!'*[11] campaign argues that the gender imbalance further sharpens the gender divide in children's reading abilities. As is often the case with diversity there are conflicting standpoints and discussions that library and information professionals need to carefully consider and then find routes to navigate through to their own satisfaction and that of their schools. Awareness of issues and discussion with others can help to inform them of ways to achieve this.

The constructions of gender referenced texts as mentioned above place male and female as binary opposites. Not everyone supports a structured approach and this can mean individuals are gender fluid, a book which explores elements of this is David Levithan's *Every Day*.

Transgender

The term 'Transgender' can be applied to those people whose sense of self-identity does not readily align with the external gender that they were assigned at birth and with societal expectations and Transsexuals often voice their wish to have gender realignment through surgery. Transgender and transsexual people frequently experience depression and anxiety due to societal pressures to conform. Assumptions are often made by society at large about sexual orientation, something which the term's inclusion in the acronym LGBT (Lesbian, Gay, Bisexual and Transgender) has contributed towards. Aidan Chambers' Carnegie winning novel of 1999, *Postcards from No Man's Land* features trans-characters. Lisa Williamson's debut novel, *The Art of Being Normal* explores trans-experiences gleaned from her time working as an administrator at the Gender Identity Development Service, an NHS service for those under 18s struggling with gender identity. Alex Gino drew upon his own experiences in penning *George*, a middle grade novel about a transgender girl Melissa who the world calls George.

Intersex

Intersex individuals are born with aspects of female and male reproductive organs. As this is physical, it is often detected by medical professions early in childhood and surgery can take place to assign a particular gender. Issues have occurred when the gender assigned at this early

---

[11] Emmett, Jonathan (2013), 'COOL not CUTE!' http://scribblestreet.co.uk/coolnotcute/COOLnotCUTE.pdf

stage of life has not matched with the mental gender that a person goes on to develop in their later years. Relatively little exploration of this problem has occurred in children's and young person's literature at the time of writing.

Key authors to look out for when exploring issues of gender include:

- Holly Bourne
- James Dawson
- Anne Fine
- Gene Kemp
- Louise O'Neill
- Meg Rosoff
- Lisa Williamson.

What to look for in books

- Do books subscribe to narrow gender stereotypes in how they are presented and marketed through use of colour and titling?
- Are a range of characters portrayed and shown with different interests, undertaking a variety of activities and holding aspirations regardless of their gender?
- Is gender conditioning and stereotyping actively probed and questioned within the books?
- Does gender stereotyping ever feel tokenistic or is this an integral part of the character and plot development?

Further reading for those interested in finding out more can be found in:

Atkinson, C. J. *Can I Tell you about Gender Diversity*, Jessica Kingsley Press.

Fine, Cordelia (2011). *Delusions of Gender: The real science behind sex differences*, Icon Books.

Flanagan, Victoria (2011). *Into the Closet*, Routledge.

Mental Health

Stigma has often been attached to mental health by many in society; research suggests that one in three young people in the UK believe that admitting to a mental health issue could affect their future job prospects.[12] Among teenagers rates of anxiety and depression have increased by a massive 70% since the mid 1980s.[13] Some of the stigma surrounding mental health arises from a lack of understanding and awareness and an assumption that people could just 'pull themselves together' or 'cheer up'. This might be a little akin to asking somebody with a broken leg to will the bones to instantly knit together and is likely to have similar levels of effect.

Although rapidly increasing, it is important to note that our general understanding of the human mind and of brain functions is still quite limited. This means that as advances in thinking and increasing knowledge of mental health occur, the language and terms that we use and the means through which this is described will alter too. What might appear acceptable and even enlightened at one date in the past might well feel misguided and even potentially harmful given the passage of time. Some of the terms from when mental health was in its infancy – feeble minded, retardation, lunatic, sub-human – whilst distasteful and offensive in the present day, did at least recognise the existence of mental conditions in past decades and centuries.

The rapid development in the science of mental health can lead to writers approaching the subject with some trepidation – uncertainty about what is acceptable to say, concerns around discussing sensitive subjects or some that might even be viewed as taboo. Visibility and presence are key ways to help break down some of these fears and ambivalences.

Whilst it is not possible to provide an exhaustive list of mental health conditions, partly because terminology and classifications are constantly changing, but also because the number of specific issues and overlaps between behaviour types and mental patterns that can occur within sets of conditions are manifold. It is also worth noting that some conditions, like personality disorders are less likely to manifest themselves until early adulthood. This section will explore some of the more prevalent conditions at young adult age and which are also reflected in literature for children and young people.

School librarians often see children and young people outside the classroom environment which means they sometimes witness more of the child's behaviour, attitudes and personality in less formal settings. This can mean that they are better placed to recognise pastoral needs that might arise from mental health conditions.

Different aspects of mental health include:

1). Wellbeing and mindfulness

Wellbeing and mindfulness are useful in achieving a more positive and happier outlook on life, finding ways to achieve mental balance. This can improve self-esteem and self-confidence. Physical activity, mental activity – stimulation of the mind and learning – connecting with people around us and being aware of our thoughts and feelings all help in achieving a sense of wellbeing and mindfulness. This can be a useful preventative measure when it comes to stress, anxiety and even depression. There are numerous books that explore issues that might be

---

[12] The Princes Trust (2017) 'Youth Index 2017' https://www.princes-trust.org.uk/Youth-Index-2017-report.pdf

[13] St John, T and McCulloch, M (2004), 'Chidhood and Adolescent Mental Health: understanding the lifetime impacts.' Mental Health Foundation

helpful to this, these include titles by Caldecott shortlisted author and illustrator Jon J Muth. Mary Hoffman has a series *'The Great Big...'* which has titles on feelings, bodies and families and covers issues relating to wellbeing and mindfulness. Many well-loved and popular children's books have innate wellbeing messages, these include David McKee's *Not Now Bernard*, Kathryn Cave's *Something Else* and more.

2). Eating Disorders

It is often the case that eating disorders are seen as having been caused by media pressure that portrays body images in a particular manner and also by social pressures from friends and family. These disorders can equally be caused by genetic and environmental factors and often arise as a result of low self-esteem, stress and control. One of the two most common eating disorders is bulimia – when an individual eats uncontrollably followed by attempting to expel this through vomiting or use of laxatives. Anorexia Nervosa, is the other eating disorder that occurs most frequently. This occurs when an individual tries to limit their weight through starvation and excessive physical exercise. Numerous titles exist for young readers about healthy eating and balanced diets; these include Alan Durant's cautionary tale, *Burger Boy*, Peter Bently's *Dustbin Dad* and Lauren Child's *I Will Not Never Ever Eat a Tomato*. For older readers there is Jean Ure's *Pumpkin Pie* and Cathy Cassidy's *Summer's Dream*. Young adult titles include Julia Bell's *Massive*, Erin Lange's *Butter* and Chris Higgins' *Perfect 10*.

3). Obsessive Compulsive Disorder

People with obsessive compulsive disorder (OCD), have frequent obsessive thoughts. These often cause anxiety and unease, and compulsive behaviours that result from these. Repetitive acts appear to provide temporary relief from the obsessive thoughts. Titles which feature OCD include Holly Bourne's *Am I Normal Yet?*, Alice Oseman's *Solitaire* and Vanessa Curtis' *One More Little Problem*.

4). Selective Mutism

This is an anxiety disorder where a person is unable or unwilling to speak in certain social situations. It often begins during childhood and can persist into adulthood. Speaking with some people in some situations can feel very stressful and can cause individuals to withdraw. Books which explore this include Laura Jarratt's *Louder than Words*, John Marsden's *So Much to Tell You*, Laurie Halse Anderson's *Speak*, Annabel Pitcher's *Silence is Goldfish* and Julie Berry's *All the Truth that's In Me*.

5). Depression

Depression is a state of feeling persistently unhappy and hopeless about one's life and life changes. It can produce a loss of interest in things that have previously contained meaning or enjoyment, and can often have associated physical symptoms – disrupted sleep patterns, fatigue, lack of appetite or libido and aches and pains. Severe depression can lead to suicidal thoughts and tendencies and a belief that life no longer has value. There are often triggers for depression such as bereavement or changes in family circumstances, but depressive tendencies can also be hereditary. Several picture books explore elements of depression for young readers, these include Levi Pinfold's *Black Dog*, Debi Gliori's *Night Shift*, Shaun Tan's *The Red Tree* and Michael

Rosen's *Sad Book*. Young adult titles that feature depression include titles by Gayle Foreman, Tabitha Suzuma and Laurie Halse Anderson, remember too *Brilliant* by Roddy Doyle.

6). Anxiety

Feelings of fear, worry and uncertainty characterise anxiety. Anxious responses encompass both emotional and physical sensations. Everyone feels anxious in different situations; however, when these feelings and responses become long-lasting, are powerful and limiting somebody's lifestyle, then there can be an underlying mental health issue. These can include physiological responses that include nausea and feeling sick, tensing of muscles and associated headaches, breathlessness, sweating, irregular heartbeat, raised blood pressure and difficulty with sleeping. There are several types of anxiety disorder:

- Generalised anxiety disorder – where a person has felt anxious for a long period but not about any issue that is easy to pinpoint – there are often many symptoms and effects to this disorder which means people's experiences can vary widely.
- Panic disorder – this is characterised by panic attacks and people experiencing these can be so fearful about having one that this anxiety itself acts as a trigger.
- Obsessive compulsive disorder (see separate section).
- Post-traumatic stress disorder – where an individual has intense feelings of anxiety following an experience or after witnessing something highly traumatic. The mind often relives this through flashbacks or nightmares.

Books that explore anxiety include Louise Gornall's *Under Rose Tinted Skies*, Ned Vizzini's *It's Kind of a Funny Story* and Catherine Forde's *Skarrs*.

Self-harm

Self-harming occurs when an individual injures or damages their body intentionally. This commonly involves the cutting or burning of skin, misuse of alcohol or drugs or punching or hitting themselves. This can be a way of finding expression for feelings and distress that are overwhelming in their intensity. Self-harm can often be indicative of other problems individuals face in their lives such as being bullied, changes in home life, other abuse, or underlying psychological issues including self-loathing and a desire to inflict punishment as a reaction. Young adult books that explore this include Patricia McCormick's *Cut*, Holly Bourne's *The Manifesto on How to Be Interesting*, and Joanne Kendrick's *Red Tears*.

Suicide

Suicidal thoughts can often arise from other mental health conditions. They can occur when problems feel overwhelming and insurmountable. Individuals, whether young or older, with suicidal thoughts or tendencies should be encouraged to talk about their problems and seek help. Clearly expert help is needed here in the quickest possible time. All threatened, attempted or suicide itself is bound to have very far reaching even devastating long-term effects on staff and students within a school environment. For fiction that explores this important issue... Anne Fine's *Up on Cloud Nine*, Jay Asher's *Thirteen Reasons Why*, Keith Gray's *The Ostrich Boys*, Andrew Norriss' *Jessica's Ghost*.

Stress

Stress occurs when people feel that they are under more emotional or mental pressure than they are able to manage and cope with. This may be related to money, low self-esteem, to pressure at home or with school work and exams. It may be short-lived or more long-lasting and can often be accompanied by associated conditions including headaches and tension. Books such as Nicola Morgan's *The Teenage Guide to Stress* and Juno Dawson's *Mind the Gap* are recommended.

Bipolar Disorder

Bipolar disorder, also known as Manic Depression is characterised by phases where the individual is likely to feel very active and positive followed by depressive phases, where individuals feel low and lethargic. Phases can last for several weeks. Bipolar Disorder is explored in Jennifer Niven's *All the Bright Places*, Jacqueline Wilson's *The Illustrated Mum*, Gwyneth Rees' *My Mum's From Planet Pluto*, Tabitha Suzuma's *A Note of Madness*.

Key authors that have explored and widened understanding of metal health and wellbeing for young people include:

- Laurie Halse Anderson
- Julia Bell
- Holly Bourne
- Juno Dawson
- Anne Fine
- Andrew Fusek Peters
- Matt Haigh
- Laura Jarratt
- Anthony McGowan
- Jon J. Muth
- Nicola Morgan
- Tabitha Suzuma
- Jacqueline Wilson.

What to look for in books

For very young children try to find books that help them to identify and better understand the range of emotions they feel – happiness, sadness, love, loneliness/separation etc. Similarly look for books that can help the reader to see difference in a positive light and for older students try to find books that cover the issue of dominance and bullying and its effects.

Consider too if mental health is looked at in a stereotypical or negative way or in a sensitive and sympathetic manner. Let's face it most of us have some sort of mental health issue sometimes in our lives.

Further Reading: Wilson, Peter (2004). *Young Minds in our Schools*, YoungMinds.

Educational Needs

Some children and young adults will find they have difficulties or disabilities which can make learning more of an obstacle for them than it is for their peers. These can include specific learning difficulties like dyslexia which cause challenges only in certain aspects of learning such as reading and writing and do not affect overall intelligence. Many children and young people with educational needs may need additional support from you as school librarian or by differentiated resources. Links with the SENCO or through the local authority Special Educational Needs Department are essential to identify and effectively provide for these pupils. It may also be useful to look at the winners of the Times Educational Supplement and National Association for Special Educational Needs (TES/NASEN) Book Award competitions.

Dyslexia

A child with dyslexia is likely to experience difficulties with reading and writing skills. It is a stable, non-degenerative condition but one that is present throughout life. It is estimated that between 10 and 20% of the United Kingdom's population has some degree of dyslexia. People with dyslexia are likely to read and write slowly, experience confusion of letter ordering in words, have poor or inconsistent spelling, put letters the wrong way round such as writing the letter 'p' instead of 'q'. Tinted gels can aid people with dyslexia so too print that is produced on cream or off white coloured paper. Barrington Stoke publisher are well known for providing materials to meet the needs of those with this condition. Their website also has useful information and support material and they have produced a 'tints' app to aid e-reading. The NUword website www.nuword.org also has valuable support and guidance including role models.

Theresa Breslin's *Whispers in the Graveyard*, features a protagonist, Solomon, with dyslexia.

Dyspraxia

Also known as developmental co-ordination disorder, children with dyspraxia are likely to experience fine and gross motor co-ordination difficulties. They may have problems with writing, additionally they may read well but not always comprehend some of the meanings in the language. Some children might be reluctant to read aloud because of non-standard articulation or low self-esteem. Titles which might be useful for dyspraxia include Anne Fine's *How to Write Really Badly* and Victoria Briggs *Caged in Chaos: A Dyspraxic Guide to Breaking Free*, written by a young person with the condition.

Attention Deficit Hyperactivity Disorder (ADHD)

Children with Attention Deficit Hyperactivity Disorder, often abbreviated to ADHD, are likely to have a limited attention span, appear very hyperactive in their behaviour and may experience difficulty in controlling their behaviour. Problems with reading often result from an inability to remember what has been read and an inability to retain information. There are strategies which can be useful in supporting children's reading. Jack Gantos has written a series about Joey Pigza, a boy with ADHD.

Titles include – *The Key that Swallowed Joey Pigza* and *I am not Joey Pigza*.

Autism

Autism is a developmental condition that affects how people perceive the world and how they communicate and relate with others. Children with autism may well struggle with reading and general language skills. Autistic children can sometimes experience difficulty decoding written instructions, but find texts with visual illustrations easier to relate to. Lesley Ely's *Looking after Louis* is a picture book that explores this common condition.

Books for older readers which explore Autistic Spectrum Disorder conditions include Kathryn Erskine's *Mockingbird*, Mark Haddon's *The Curious Incident of the Dog in the Night-Time*, Kim Slater's *Smart*, Siobhan Dowd's *The London Eye Mystery* and Ann M. Martin's *How to Look for a Lost Dog*.

For further information do have a look at:
National Literacy Trust – *Ideas: Encouraging Children with Special Educational needs to enjoy reading.* http://www.literacytrust.org.uk/resources/practical_resources_info/3129_resource-ideas_encouraging_children_with_special_educational_needs_to_enjoy_reading

Religion

In the Judaeo-Christian world, many early stories found in children's literature can be traced back to early texts focusing on religious tracts and instruction. It can be the case that different systems of belief have tensions between them that could well be historic, based on a conflict of place or law or prejudice – believing that one system is correct and other systems of lesser value or worth. There has been a long history of belief systems coming into conflict with one another – one immediately thinks of the current Palestine issues and or in an earlier civilisation, the ideas outlined by Socrates or in the late 16th century and early 17th century the conflict between the Protestants and Roman Catholics and indeed Galileo's views of the universe which were viewed as heretical at the time by the Roman Catholic church.

Social exclusion, cultural inferiority, social disorders

Failure to address, understand and respect differences in faith can lead to hostility and persecution. Literature can be used as a vehicle of hate – titles can be politicised in attempts to indoctrinate new generations into cultures of hostility, fear and hatred of others One thinks of the rise of anti-Semitic literature in Germany before and during the Second World War when the written word was one of several instruments used to disseminate messages of bigotry and intolerance against Jews and other minority groups.

Anti-semitism has a long history in books accessible to young people. One thinks immediately of Shakespeare's Shylock in *The Merchant of Venice* and Dickens' Fagin in *Oliver Twist*. The stereotype of Jews as money-lenders, used by Shakespeare, is appropriated in Nesbit's *Story of the Treasure Seekers* with Mr Rosenbaum. It remains difficult to find children's literature in the UK which represents Jewish concerns that are not focussed specifically on or around the aftermath of the Holocaust, such as Sharon Dogar's *Annexed*.

Islamophobia is another key area where religious persecution occurs in the current world. Since 9/11 in 2001 and latterly the events surrounding ISIS or IS, there has been a tendency, particularly among some far-right organisations, to assume Islam and Terrorism are synonymous which of course they are not. The Department for Education has released guidance for schools 'Protecting children from radicalisation'[14] in an attempt to help teachers, school librarians and others to overcome these tensions.

Religious sensitivities can mean there are some titles and themes that are probably best avoided. Some Church schools avoid titles featuring any kind of witchcraft. Those of the Jehovah Witness faith often avoid subjects relating to the paranormal. Muslim and Jewish schools may avoid titles relating to pigs.

To find out more read:

Madelyn Travis, (2013), *Jews and Jewishness in British Children's Literature*, Routledge

Key authors include Alan Gibbons, Elizabeth Laird, Bali Rai.

---

[14] (2015) Protecting Children from Radicalisation: the prevent duty'
https://www.gov.uk/government/publications/protecting-children-from-radicalisation-the-prevent-duty

Things to look out for

■ Do characters of certain religions appear in a way that feel stereotyped?

■ Do characters feel ciphers for religion only?

■ Is one religion or system of belief given predominance over another?

■ Does the author appear even handed when creating scenes concerning religious conflicts or actions?

Race

In our trans-global society where language, ideas and people themselves are able to shift between geographical areas with ease and swiftness, we need to ensure that children's literature reflects the backgrounds, experiences and current preoccupations that face our students of different cultures. We currently need to give young people access to lots of texts that relate to the diaspora of different cultures, the dispersal of people from beyond their homeland and the wider issues of identity and migration.

It's important to remember that dominant narratives in children's literature available in the United Kingdom have historically tended to relate only to the UK white experience. Where other cultures or races were explored in more historic titles, this has often served a narrative function rather than being a primary focus. The Indian setting and characters in Frances Hodgson Burnett's *The Secret Garden* written in 1911, provide a sense of exoticism with which the 'down-to-earth' values of Yorkshire are contrasted. It's important to realise that there has been an inadvertent tendency over past decades for the experiences and lifestyles of different races and cultures to be related only by white authors and illustrators perhaps due to a hangover of ideas of Empire and the rather narrow demographic of publishing. Editors might have inherently looked for what they know, or perhaps because some cultural groups do not have equal representation in the publishing world.

A further possible reason could be the different set of tropes and traditions associated with how storytelling operates in cultures. Whatever the reasons it seems that there wasn't always an understanding of these differences in cultures and the range of books on school library shelves could usefully have been much wider.

In the 1970s and 1980s different racial voices began to be published in the children's sector with authors like Farukkh Dhondy, James Berry and Jamila Gavin and illustrator Errol Lloyd as particularly notable examples. Their work actively reflected the cultures and traditions specific to different communities. In spite of this, there is still a general under-representation both in terms of what is published and also, by consequence, in associated critical and promotional activities – reviews, reading initiatives and awards of different cultural groups, their aspirations and challenges in UK children's publishing.

Racism

Racism occurs when a group of people is not treated equally based on their ethnic origins or skin colour. Manifesting itself through actions, words, thinking or behaviour, it may be conscious or subconscious and may be embedded in a set of societal or institutional practices. Viewpoints that are driven by race can easily fall prey to becoming discriminatory. Clashes of stance between different races and cultural standpoints can be difficult to reconcile. The politically charged atmosphere that followed 9/11 in 2001 saw race riots occur in several towns of Northern England such as Burnley and Oldham. There are many books, factual and fictional, which recount this conflict, titles like Richard MacSween's *Victory Street* or Alan Gibbons *Caught in the Crossfire* come to mind. They explore ways that cultures can be segregated and also importantly, ways in which rifts can be healed.

The issues and sensitivities of racial issues are growing more complex as cultures and people increasingly interact and relate to each other. This means that our racial awareness has to be ever more educated and sensitive. The way that stories concerning some races and cultural groups are written and portrayed are sometimes queried – does the author have enough knowledge or is he/she sufficiently embedded in that cultural background? It's easy to assume a level of understanding and empathy with works by writers of ethnic origins about their own culture, but it is also worth remembering there is no single perspective or universal experience when writing. If possible Young People need to be offered and be able to read a variety of titles about each and all cultures.

As we all know war, politics and economic factors drive people to move beyond their homelands. We currently have serious coverage of migration and immigration in the UK in the news and national press. There are numerous books that explore migration and offer counter-balance to the skewed perspective that the popular media sometimes expounds. One racial or cultural group or another often appear to be within their sights. Individuals from the Gypsy, Roma and Traveller communities often experience considerable racial prejudice and stereotyping too. Titles like Rumer Godden's *Diddakoi*, Siobhan Dowd's *The Pavee and the Buffer Man* and Cathy Cassidy's *Dizzy* relate some aspects of Traveller experience, but it remains a relatively under-represented area.

Key authors include John Agard, Malorie Blackman, Sita Brahmachari, Jamila Gavin, Liam Hearne, Irfan Master, Ifeoma Onyefulu, Bali Rai, S. F. Said, Gene Luen Yang, Benjamin Zephaniah.

Things to look out for in books

- Do different cultures assimilate into the way of life in the United Kingdom?
- What does it mean if they do and does this represent the domination of one set of traditions and values over another?
- Is there a sense in which culture needs to be preserved and, if so, how can this be achieved? Dual language books, titles in translation, Marsh Award for Literature, BookTrust translation project.

If you want to find out more try reading:

Chaudhri, Amina, (2017), *Multiracial Identity in Children's Literature*, Routledge.

Gonzales, Macarena Garcia, (2017), *Origin Narratives: The Stories We Tell Children About Immigration and International Adoption*, Routledge.

Visual impairment

Where eyesight is limited in function or may not operate occurs in a substantial number of children. Pupils with visual impairments may need access to large print copies or magnifiers. In more profound cases it may be that audio editions or braille or moon editions are useful. Tactile picture books can also be useful for younger children and are becoming more prevalent with 3D printing.

As already suggested on page 11, do contact the RNIB and Calibre for further support and advice, training and resources.

Section 2: Creating a Diverse Approach to Library Stock and Services

Consider Your Users

One of the first tasks in taking a diverse approach to the school library or learning resource centre is to scope your users – analyse your users, their reading habits and identifying their needs and the key issues that arise with regard to provision of library stock on the shelves.

Consider –

- Diversity of users
- Diversity of reading habits
- Diversity of your collection of materials on offer to your students and young people.

It is useful to remember that although there may only be a small number of a particular group of people in your school community it is still important to represent their issues and beliefs as part of your role as librarian. As part of this process, it is useful to try to reflect on the number of those users that actively use the library and those that do not. Are there any groups of people that consistently do not use the library and are there reasons why that might be the case?

Stock Audits

- Where gaps are there and why? (Perhaps finance is a serious issue for you.)
- Does the available material on your shelves reflect views or attitudes that are now outdated?
- Are the needs of all possible users being met?
- Looking through your stock, which would you classify as being diverse and why? It might also be useful to consider the background and origins of the authors themselves to ensure that a balance of viewpoints are represented.
- You might find it useful to use the **'What to look for sections'** under the categories of diversity explored within Section One of this publication. These may also be useful in helping to appraise potential new stock.

Cordelia Fine discusses the importance of measures as part of diversity in her comments in Section 4.

Collection Development Policy

Do think about the various ways in which you can ensure that diversity is reflected in the collection.

- This might include deciding on core stock – titles which you feel are so important that they should always be stocked by the library.
- If there are particular authors that you feel are useful in representing diversity consider

adding them as standing order items so that should/when they publish a new title, this automatically gets added to your order list.

- The Diversity policy will also ideally consider provision of works in translation, works in different print sizes, audio editions and dual language editions.

- Consider the collection as a whole. Does it represent and reflect a wide range of different lifestyles and backgrounds.

- As well as considering titles in their own right, regarding their age and interest suitability and their production values, consider the collection as a whole and where items might fit on the shelves and the needs they fulfil. A challenge with diversity is the emergent nature of publishers' approaches to different facets of diversity. This can mean that sourcing material is not easy – titles may not be in print and so might not be immediately or readily available. It might be necessary therefore to seek quality second-hand titles. Abebooks, Amazon Marketplace and even Ebay can be useful in sourcing these and of course contact your usual recognised and established suppliers for advice on obtaining titles.

The offer to school libraries

From nursery to sixth form, there are a number of very professional and expert book suppliers such as Askews and Holts Library Services, Brown's Books of Students, Peters and others who help schools across the UK to make efficient use of their budgets and choose the best stock for their needs.

Hazel Holmes from Askews writes

Our multiple copy showroom, holding approximately 150,000 volumes of children's junior fiction and non-fiction material, with all core authors and new titles, suitable for school libraries.

We stock curriculum related topics suitable for all Key Stages, as well as specialist publications. We actively encourage teachers and librarians to visit our showroom to discuss their needs with our schools services staff. Their experience in the book trade and knowledge of the schools market enables them to advise visitors on stock selection. However, if a visit to our showroom isn't convenient, our market leading website provides access to subjects covered within the National Curriculum and for ease of selection topic box and key stage lists of titles are displayed and refreshed on a regular basis. In addition, we supply lists of new titles, bespoke online subject lists and physical themed collections, based around the curriculum.

To prepare stock for library use, we also offer a full range of book processing options. These include jacketing, security triggers, RFID, barcodes, ownership labels and date labels. A supplier selection service is also offered to schools and schools library services. VLeBooks, Askews and Holts' eBook service for Further Education and Higher Education Institutions was launched in 2013 and has proven to be hugely popular with both librarians and students alike, with the platform being voted, by students, as the most user-friendly eBook service in a number of institutions.

For the library, multiple licence options and hands-on eBook management tools provide the necessary flexibility and scope to ensure that titles are always available for students, particularly during peak usage times.

The student can either read online, using our bespoke online reader or download the eBook to their devices. Online reading offers many additional tools to assist the student in their studies, for example, printing a range of pages and note sharing.

In terms of Reader Development, we have an array of resources available on our website. These include Subject Lists, Promotional Collections, Book Club Guides, Author Interviews and our bi-monthly Adult and Children's Newsletters.

Commitment to Diversity:

We have recently signed the Everybody In Charter and are committed to ensuring that children can find authentic representations of themselves and those that are different in the books we supply. We work closely with publishers to ensure inclusiveness is something that is valued and pushed to the forefront of new publishing.

Assessing Diversity:

We assess titles individually before selecting and try to avoid anything with damaging stereotypes, although this is happening much less frequently. Publishers and authors are very aware of the impact their characters are having on their readers. A realistic portrayal of 'diverse' characters and lives is becoming ever more important. Race, heritage, disability, gender, sexual orientation, age, religion, social status and culture are all aspects that are considered, and we are seeing these factors much more in mainstream publishing, especially LGBT issues in YA.

Good Practice:

Some authorities have also signed Everybody In Charter and requested that we are conscious of inclusion whilst completing supplier selections.

Suggestions for Schools

To broaden their appeal some new, smaller and independent publishers focus their publishing schedule quite heavily on diversity but because they are relatively unknown they can often be overlooked by busy school librarians.[15] As I suggested earlier sometimes questions can be raised about authenticity of voice and a given author's right to tell a particular story or relate to a culture. It is often difficult for school library staff to make informed decisions about this issue. For this reason it can sometimes be useful to consult with your young people themselves about the types of resources that they feel best meet their needs. If your users can be actively involved in the decision making process, they are more likely to feel a sense of ownership over the library and the collection and to act as champions and advocates for it in all its diversity.

Acquisitions from smaller publishers

Many smaller publishers produce materials and content that reflect different community and cultural needs. These smaller, often independent publishers are often well placed to know their

---

15 Holmes, Hazel (2017), Personal Correspondence [31/03/2017]

market and connect with them; however, it can be the case that their publications don't always have the quality of writing as older more established publishing houses. Do consider images portrayed on dust sleeves or even rebinding of quality titles to extend shelf life.

Remember to consult your local School Library Service and your public library service when you need help for particular children or families.

BookTrust and the Letterbox Library both have useful websites which can offer support for current knowledge and awareness of new and forthcoming titles.

Controversies

Creating a written collection development policy within an overall school library policy document can help to ensure that if challenges to your choice of material arises, then there is a written statement to support your thinking that is agreed and supported by your line manager and perhaps your head teacher too. A policy can help you to explain why and how you have specific titles on your shelves to support the reading and information needs of your users.

Sometimes controversies arise over particular diverse titles. One title that often raises discussion is Herge's *Tintin in the Congo*. A precursor to the immensely popular graphic novel series starring the eponymous, quiffed journalist, this title features colonial views of Africa both in terms of the text of the story and in terms of the visual depictions presented in the illustrations themselves. This caused controversy in 2007 when the Commission for Racial Equality branded the book racist with a spokesperson claiming *'This book contains imagery and words of hideous racial prejudice, where the 'savage natives' look like monkeys and talk like imbeciles.'*[16] Ann Widdecombe at that time an M.P., felt the comments made by the commission brought 'the CRE into disrepute – there are many more serious things for them to worry about' she stated. These polarised views are difficult to accommodate. What is the correct decision to make in such circumstances? How would (or did) you respond? It's worth considering the nature and range of the objections. There can be a tendency to pillory authors and illustrators for not having held attitudes that would have been conventional or very forward-thinking for the time. The more recent controversy in Oxford about Cecil Rhodes being a case in point.

Questions to ask can be:

- What is the value or worth of potentially contentious items to the collection – in terms of the role they are able to play in encouraging a culture of reading for pleasure or disseminating information and knowledge of different cultures and groups to children and young people?

- What other types of resource are present that help to counter balance the attitudes found within the item?

- Can you display resources that show or hold different viewpoints together? How can you present the resources and their content in a way that opens up discussion and debate?

- Do you have a firm rationale for removing the item from the shelves in line with your Collections Policy?

---

[16] Beckford, Martin (12 July, 2007) 'Ban 'racist' Tintin book, says CRE',
http://www.telegraph.co.uk/news/uknews/1557233/Ban-racist-Tintin-book-says-CRE.html Martin Beckford,
12 July 2007 The Telegraph

Section 3: Reading Development

Diverse titles might need a greater push and more vigorous promotion than others. Do consider if they can be included in displays, whether there are ways to actively encourage greater use through your own recommendation or peer recommendation. Reading groups can form a valuable way through which to introduce children and young people to diversity and help them to explore some of the issues and challenges arising from this. The mediated nature of reading groups also means it is possible to frame and present issues so that ethical exploration is also considered. Author, illustrator, storyteller or poet visits can be another useful and high profile way to help generate interest in diverse titles. Hearing an artist speak directly will often bring about a surge of interest and engagement with their works and a well-placed display of thematically related titles can build and stimulate further interest and involvement.

Cultural Calendar of Events

Link your diversity titles to a yearly cycle of events – it's always useful to link to national and local coverage of specific events. For example, the University of Portsmouth produces a diversity calendar that will give you many ideas across the year:
http://www.port.ac.uk/departments/services/equalityanddiversity/diversitycalendar/

Many annual days and events are widely celebrated and supported by resources and information available electronically. It is probably advisable to select a small number of these to recognise and to draw particular focus to particular themes or issues that are topical or that have relevance in your school and students. Clearly it's useful to link with colleagues in subject departments and to encourage students to become involved in helping to design and shape the various activities and promotions. Many of the focus days have application through citizenship, history, geography, and biology.

Highlights across the year

International Holocaust Memorial Day

27 January

This is an annual commemoration of the victims of the Holocaust, recognising the genocide of approximately 6 million Jewish people, 2 million Romany people, and others who were mentally and physically disabled, who were persecuted because of their sexuality or their political views. It marks the liberation of Auschwitz-Birkenau, the largest of the concentration camps under the Nazi regime. In addition to commemorating victims of the Holocaust, it seeks to recognise other genocide attempts across the world. There is a dedicated website which provides resources, background and ideas for activity – http://hmd.org.uk/

Lesbian Gay Bisexual and Trans History Month

February

This aims to educate young people against prejudice. The event is usually themed to help provide focus and a variety of online resources are available via the official website – lgbthistorymonth.org.uk

World Day of Social Justice

20 February

Organised by the United Nations, this day is intended to raise awareness about exclusion and inequality and aims to ensure people are able to have chances to improve their lives and those around them without barriers of age, race, ethnicity, religion, culture or disability. Information about the day can be found on the United Nations website – www.un.org

World Book Day

First Thursday in March

This is a celebration of books and reading. In the UK it is held on the first Thursday in March. There are opportunities to focus upon books and authors from around the world – www.worldbookday.com

International Women's Day

8 March

IWD is a global celebration of the social, economic, political and cultural achievements made by women. In addition to creating recognition for women's achievements, it also aims to advocate and champion gender equality. The day is themed and a dedicated website offers resources, background and material – https://www.internationalwomensday.com/

International Day for the Elimination of Racial Discrimination

21 March

A focus day for racism and a way to fight any kind of racial discrimination. The event is organised by the United Nations and is themed. Information and background can be found on the United Nations website – www.un.org

World Autism Awareness Day

2 April

An annual date when autism organisations celebrate and raise awareness of Autism and aspirations and opportunities for those who are Autistic and raise funds for research into this condition. More information can be found at Autism Speaks – https://www.autismspeaks.org/what-autism/world-autism-awareness-day

World Health Day

7 April

Organised by the World Health Organisation, it is held to mark the founding of the organisation and provides an opportunity to draw attention to major global health issues. The date is themed and resources and background to the annual themes can be found on the World Health Organisation website – http://www.who.int/campaigns/world-health-day/2017/en/

International Day Against Homophobia, Transphobia and Biphobia

17 May

Hailed as a celebration of worldwide sexual and gender diversities, the day was established to draw the attention of policymakers, leaders, social movements, the media and the public at large to the ongoing discrimination and violence experienced by lesbian, gay, bisexual, trans and intersex people across the globe. The day is themed and is supported through a dedicated website which contains background and information against homophobia – http://dayagainsthomophobia.org/

World Day for Cultural Diversity for Dialogue and Development

21 May

This day, organised by the United Nations, is intended to promote understanding of the values of cultural diversity and the influence and impact it is able to make to the creative industry and as an accelerant for sustainable development. More information can be found at http://www.un.org/en/events/culturaldiversityday/

Gypsy Roma Traveller History Month

June

Britain has a history of Gypsies, Roma and Traveller communities living, working and travelling throughout the land for over 500 years, but their part in our history is not widely recognised. This month has been established to help remedy that. More information about the initiative and a range of insightful articles and information can be found at http://grthm.natt.org.uk/index.php

World Refugee Day

20 June

A date to promote public awareness and allegiance with refugees, seeking to ensure every refugee child has access to an education, that refugee families have a safe place in which to live and have opportunities to work or to learn skills to make a positive contribution to their community. Organised by the United Nations, there is further information on their website – http://www.un.org/en/events/refugeeday/

World Suicide Prevention Day

10 September

Organised by the International Association for Suicide Prevention, the day is a response to the World Health Organisation's estimate that in excess of 800,000 people die by suicide each year. The day is intended to raise awareness about mental health issues and suicide behaviour, with the intention of saving lives. Further information can be found on the International Association for Suicide Prevention website – https://iasp.info/wspd2017/

European Day of Languages

26 September

A day of events and activities that is aimed at encouraging learning more languages at any age both in and outside school. The intention is that linguistic diversity is a tool for understanding and a rich part of the cultural heritage of Europe. Further information can be found at http://edl.ecml.at/

International Translation Day

30 September

Celebrated annually on the feast of St Jerome, the translator of the bible. Organised by the International Federation of Translators, it is themed and an electronic poster is produced each year. Further information can be found at Free Word Centre – https://www.freewordcentre.com/explore/projects/international-translation-day

Black History Month

October

This is themed and very well resourced on the official website which features case-studies of key figures and pioneers, diversity champions of the movement and also includes an image bank – www.blackhistorymonth.org.uk

World Cerebral Palsy Day

First Wednesday each October

This intends to raise awareness of issues that affect people with Cerebral Palsy, helping us all to strive for a more inclusive approach. Further information and resources are available on a dedicated website – https://worldcpday.org/

World Mental Health Day

10 October

It is a themed day the aim of which is to raise awareness and to help break down some of the stigma about mental health. Supported by the World Health Organisation, a range of resources and information can be sourced on their website – www.who.int

Transgender Awareness Week

1–14 November

Despite its name, this is an event held over a fortnight that leads to Transgender Day of Remembrance (20 November) which commemorates victims of transphobic violence. The aims for the day are to educate the general public about transgender and gender non-conforming people as well as the issues associated with transition and identity. Organised by GLAAD (formerly the Gay and Lesbian Alliance Against Defamation). Further information about both dates is available on the GLAAD website – www.glaad.org

International Day for Tolerance

16 November

Organised by the United Nations, the date is intended to remind us to show a commitment to strengthening tolerance through encouraging mutual understanding among different cultures and people. Further information can be found on the United Nations website – http://www.un.org/en/events/toleranceday/

World AIDS Day

1 December

Here is an opportunity to support people living with HIV and to commemorate those who have died as a consequence of it. Hailed as the first global health day, it was first held in 1988. Further information and resources can be found on the dedicated website – https://www.worldaidsday.org/

International Day for the Abolition of Slavery

2 December

Held to recognise the date of adoption for the United Nations Convention for the Suppression of the Traffic in Persons and of the Exploitation of the Prostitution of Others. The date is organised by the United Nations and further information can be found on their website – http://www.un.org/en/events/slaveryabolitionday/

International Day of Persons with Disabilities

3 December

A themed day organised by the United Nations, it is celebrated across the globe and is intended to champion equal participation in society of persons with disability. Further information can be found on the United Nations website – http://www.un.org/en/events/disabilitiesday/

Human Rights Day

10 December

Held to commemorate the adoption of the Universal Declaration of Human Rights, the event is organised by the United Nations and advocates the rights of all individuals whatever their geographic location or social position. Further information can be found on the United Nations website – http://www.un.org/en/events/humanrightsday/

Section 4: Case Studies

The case studies below give some examples of projects and activities that promote and encourage thinking about diversity. Hopefully they will provide you with ideas for your own work.

Case Study 1
Shared Reading Groups

Background

Reading groups have long provided an environment where participants have been able to share experiences, interpretations of a text and emotions. Carefully chosen texts can offer opportunities for the articulation of often complex feelings and situations. The shared reading model takes this as its base, but enables the act of reading and encountering the text itself to be shared through reading aloud.

Aim

To provide a safe forum for the expression of emotions and experience. To facilitate discussion and to allow participation regardless of overall reading ability and confidence.

Resources Needed

A neutral, safe space where the group can meet without interruption and in relative comfort.

To aid informality it is ideal if refreshments, drinks and cakes, can be provided so that this feels distinct from a class activity and so that participants can feel as relaxed and at ease as possible thereby stimulating their involvement and participation.

The selection of texts should be made beforehand – often shorter texts like poems or short stories will work particularly well as there is a sense of completion and resolution in the piece which the group can appreciate in a single session.

Ideally all participants should have access to the text so multiple copies are needed.

Project Outline

Consider the number of participants that will be involved – as always group size and group number need thoughtful planning depending on the age range of the participants. Clearly younger and older children are likely to be at different developmental stages and have different empathic responses and levels of emotional sophistication.

Selection of the texts is key – short enough that they can be read and explored in a single session. Matched to interest age and ability level, these also need to provide effective opportunities for discussion. Texts that make us think and empathise are likely to work well, if you have a positive response, that's a very useful starting point.

It's worthwhile considering how long the sessions will be and whether you will break for refreshments. Often this can be a good idea as it can help to keep participants on track and upbeat.

Outcomes

As the texts are read aloud, they may well provide an access point to stories and writing for those who feel lacking in confidence when reading. Careful selection of texts can act as a catalyst, helping to engage and motivate. The sessions can also be a useful way to discuss feelings and emotions and so raise empathic responses.

Case Study 2
Diverse Voices

Background

The Diverse Voices Award and reading promotion grew out of the Diversity Matters Conference of 2006 which saw professionals from the publishing industry, from libraries and teaching come together to explore the challenges facing the publication and use of culturally diverse children's books. Frances Lincoln publishers were keen to establish an award that would help create a platform for new writers who were committed to reflecting diversity through their work, or whose background was itself culturally diverse. The publisher joined with Seven Stories: The Centre for the Children's Book in Newcastle, who ably provided project management and administrative support.

This was followed by a debate to identify 50 top children's books that were culturally diverse at the time in an effort to show the progress made in children's publishing and thus make clearer and give context to some of the challenges still ahead.

Aim

To address the under-representation of both culturally diverse characters in contemporary children's fiction and also to stimulate writing and publication by authors from a culturally diverse background.

To identify 50 influential culturally diverse children's books published in the United Kingdom and to stimulate interest and promotion of these titles as a means for providing context for the development of the field.

Project Outline

The competition ran four times and resulted in the publication of nine culturally diverse children's books. When Frances Lincoln became a part of the Quarto Publishing Group, priorities changed resulting in a promotion to identify 50 children's books that had been key in reflecting cultural diversity.

For this section a panel of experts were drawn together that represented publishing, reading promotion, libraries and reviewers.

The selection was drawn up from a longlist of titles nominated by publishers, suggested by a panel and put forward through research. Titles were selected to ensure representation of different cultures and ethnic groups and to allow a spread across different age ranges, interest ranges and ability levels. Books were read and championed by the panellists and decisions made as to which constituted the most influential titles.

An announcement was held at The Guardian offices and a feature was printed in the newspaper. Seven Stories developed educational support materials which were tested with a range of groups and classes. Further information and resources are available on the Seven Stories website http://www.sevenstories.org.uk/

Outcomes

The competition saw nine culturally diverse books published by Seven Stories. The promotion drew together a recommended list which has been used for promotions in schools and in library settings. This is supported by a range of educational support materials.

Create your own activity based on this work:

Resources Needed

Identify from your own shelves a collection of your own best loved and most recognised diversity books – perhaps relating to some of the dates outlined above.

Case Study 3
Library of Lives

Background

The publishing industry is not always responsive to social changes and needs and it may be that there are times when you cannot source books or content that you feel matches the needs of the school and reflects the needs and aspirations of the wider community.

The Library of Lives may offer a model that is able to better reflect this. It takes as its premise the idea that every individual has his/her own unique story that has grown out of their experiences and background and that sometimes we are the best people to be able to relate that – to interact and to offer insight into our own unique perspectives through connection and conversation.

It can be a low cost, but very engaging way to promote the local diverse backgrounds and lifestyles of people we know and others in the community. Individuals with stories to tell become 'living books' that people can 'borrow', listen to and having the chance to interact with and hopefully to better understand their experiences and help to broaden our own.

Aim

To encourage people to share elements of their lives and to increase understanding and empathy through direct contact. To encourage and facilitate greater community cohesion through lively and interactive short talks.

Resources Needed

A range of willing participants to act as the living 'books'.

A large space where our people/'books' can be given dedicated areas. Depending on space available, this might work well in the library or perhaps the school hall.

Posters to recruit for living 'books' who would be willing to tell their stories. It may also be worthwhile to send letters home to encourage interest from parents, carers and family members.

A leaflet, or catalogue, detailing the 'books' available, these should be photocopied so that attendees can have copies and make their selection.

A booking system to keep track of which people 'books' your borrowers would like to engage with. It is a good idea to allow ten minutes per booking.

Refreshments will always be welcome – ideally for both the living 'books' and the borrowers.

Project Outline

1. Select a date and time slot for the event to take place – generally a period of two or three hours works well. You might like to consider selecting a day that matches one of the dates listed in your Diversity calendar. This model can work well with a range of different types of people 'books', or it can be focused more on different experiences that fall under a particular theme such as – different types of lives, careers and challenges that women have had as part

of International Women's Day – this could work well in a school setting by focussing on alumni – or experiences of LGBT individuals during February for LGBT History month.

2. Having arranged your date and venue, next arrange your living 'books'. Between twelve and fifteen makes for a good event and ideally these people should represent a range of different perspectives, experiences and views. You might find it useful to look at section one of the 'book' which reflects some of the diversity groups you have chosen to consider.

3. Posters, sessions in assembly and letters home to parents and carers advising family members who can be invited to participate. Your guests will need to be sensitive to the fact and comfortable that they will be sharing their experiences/stories which may be quite personal and reflective with children or young people.

4. When there are a good number of individuals interested in taking part as 'books', brief them thoroughly and sensitively as to the needs of the audience – this can be done in person, via telephone or e-mail – to decide on the focus of their story and also to give it a title. Having a record of these is key as this will form the basis for the Library of Lives catalogue, a leaflet that lists all of the names, titles and gives a short outline of what the 'book' is about, this will help people to choose the books/experiences they are most interested to learn about.

5. It is also worth letting the 'books' know that they should prepare roughly the types of areas they are happy to speak about. The sessions work best if borrowers are able to ask questions and are more effective if a little time can be set aside at the end of each session for dialogue and discussion between 'borrower' and 'book'.

6. Once the catalogue is put together, you might like to outline your 'books' before the event so that there are opportunities for your young people to express interest and so that the event itself can benefit from some word of mouth promotion before it occurs. It is worth thinking about who your intended audience is.

7. Hopefully you will have decided on your audience – these could be those involved in a PSHE lesson, or alternatively could be taken off timetable. It may be that you decide to hold this as a lunchtime or after school session, making it available to students, parents and carers alike.

8. On the day make sure that each person 'book' has a dedicated space of their own with a couple of spare chairs for borrowers to use – sometimes borrowers like to attend in couples and this can feel less intimidating, but it is worth checking with the living 'books' they are happy and feel comfortable with that arrangement.

It is a good idea to have some volunteers to help welcome borrowers that attend and to make sure that living 'books' are aware of when they have sessions. It is also important to have someone at an enquiry desk who can complete bookings and be an immediate point of contact for either borrowers or living 'books' alike.

Outcomes

Raising awareness about the types of contemporary experiences that people in the community have had, giving a voice to people that might sometimes be marginalised.

Case Study 4

Multicultural Rhyme times – for very young children

Background

Children from a very young age respond to rhymes both physically and emotionally. Nursery rhymes occur in many different cultures and these can be shared in translation of the original languages. This can be a great way to bring together parents and carers from a range of different cultures. This is best aimed at children in reception or nursery.

Aim

To introduce children from an early age to people from different backgrounds and to share other languages and cultural experiences.

Resources Needed

Adequate space – your school library.

A range of simply instruments – drums, tambourines, maracas, shakers, bells etc.

Photocopies of rhymes from different culture.

Project Outline

Invite parents and carers to contribute nursery rhymes from different cultures from their own background or that of others. Do remember to ask for a rough translation of the rhyme's meaning in English and an idea of the tune it is sung to – this can be provided in MP3 form through singing or humming if that makes it easier.

Host a multicultural rhyme time using these nursery rhymes and encourage children to take part through singing and using basic instruments. This can be followed up with a storytime with a book that has been chosen that shows one of the host countries of the rhymes.

A simple map can also be created as a display that plots all of the different places across the world from where rhymes have come.

A promotion of picture books set in other countries or cultures can also be produced to support this work.

If you are able to produce a booklet of the rhymes, this can be something that parents and teachers can support/reinforce/enjoy after the event.

Outcomes

Greater awareness of cultural differences and similarities and parental involvement. Awareness of different links that the children in the class have across the world.

Case Study 5

A Change is Gonna Come

Background

In August 2017 Stripes Publishing published a Young Adult anthology of short fiction and poetry from Black Asian and Minority Ethnic (BAME) backgrounds entitled *A Change is Gonna Come*. An open call for submissions was held for unpublished and unagented writers of short stories responding to the theme of change. Judges included agent Julia Kingsford, online editor of The Bookseller and co-founder of the BAME in Publishing network Sarah Shaffi and Stripes editorial staff.

Aim

To showcase the range and wealth of writing talent from BAME backgrounds. To provide a platform for introduced new talent and writing.

Resources Needed

It is unlikely this is replicable, as the output is a publication.

Outcomes

This anthology brings together four new voices, Mary Bello, Aisha Bushby, Yasmin Rahman and Phoebe Roy, making their work available alongside work by established authors including Tanya Byrne, Inua Ellams, Catherine Johnson, Patrice Lawrence, Ayisha Malik, Irfan Master, Nikesh Shukla and Lemn Sissay. This is a useful book for introducing a variety of cultural experiences and stand-points and acts as a taster for work by an exciting range of authors and poets.

See details at http://www.littletiger.co.uk/tiger-blog/a-change-is-gonna-come

Section 5:
Organisations that promote Diversity

BookTrust

BookTrust is the UK's largest reading charity. It reaches approximately 2.5 million children across the United Kingdom with its range of initiatives, books and support materials. The organisation's aim is to inspire a love of reading and it runs numerous programmes that provide books and reading resources for children with additional needs.

Collaborating with Publisher Child's Play International Ltd., BookTrust have been able to develop three titles as Board books in conjunction with families and organisations working with blind and partially-sighted children. *Off to the Park, Off to the Beach* and *Getting Ready* for toddlers and very young children.

See details at http://www.childs-play.com/bookshop/9781846435027.html

The organisation also holds separate book selections for Bookbuzz and the School Library Pack titles which go into special schools. Titles are selected to reflect and address a range of different learning needs, ensuring that all children are able to access books and see themselves represented.

BookTrust are also working with publishers from around the globe, inviting them to submit books that have not yet been translated into English. This is part of a new initiative called 'In Other Words'. Ten titles will be selected and partial translations will be commissioned before being presented to the UK publishing community. The initiative is intended to encourage British publishers to buy more books in from other countries and territories and, through translation, improve the diversity and widen cultural perspectives available in books published here.

Do also see the SLA's *A World of Books in Translation* in the Riveting Reads series. This is an annotated selection of superb titles suitable for the Under 8s to the 14+ age range.

Inclusive Minds

Comprised from a range of consultants and campaigners, Inclusive Minds, with a strap line of *'Working together to change the face of children's literature'*, is an organisation advocating for inclusive, diverse and accessible children's literature that embodies and champions equality.

This organisation works with writers, illustrators, publishers, librarians, teachers, booksellers and experts and practitioners working in the field of children's books and reading to design and deliver projects that seek to create diverse, inclusive and accessible books for children and young people.

One of the major challenges in this work is embedding diversity, inclusion and equality into classroom and school library practices. With that in mind, this group has developed a charter 'Everybody In' to help build critical mass for and sustainability in these matters.

See details at http://www.inclusiveminds.com/everybody-in-charters.php

Further information on Inclusive Minds including details about their projects and campaigning and a valuable spotlight which draws attention to key titles and conversations about these issues can be found at www.inclusiveminds.com.

Letterbox Library

The Letterbox Library was founded in 1983 by two single mums who recognised the power of books and stories to influence their children's lives. They decided to set up a company that would promote and make available books that were not generally available in high street stores and that better reflected the lives and experiences of children growing up and that promoted diversity and equality.

The Letterbox Library offers a range of several hundred children's books through their catalogue and website and seeks to ensure that the titles they select:

- showcase and positively reflect the diversity of communities within the United Kingdom and across the globe
- reflect multicultural society
- reflect in both text and illustrations people and groups that are often under-represented in children's literature – ethnic groups, refugees, migrants, faith groups, children with diverse family make-ups and who have different physical and learning needs
- challenge gender stereotypes and gendered assumptions
- offer opportunities to explore a range of personal and social issues relating to families, citizenship and the environment.

The Letter Box Library also administers the Little Rebels Children's Book Award which recognises works of radical fiction for children aged between 0 to 12. Further information can be found on the award blog https://littlerebelsaward.wordpress.com

For more information about the Letterbox Library and to keep up to date with their services and stock, visit www.letterboxlibrary.com.

The Letterbox Club (a part of the Letterbox Library) gives books to children in care. Children looked after in care often have lower educational attainment levels than their peers. Letterbox Club parcels can help improve reading, but also ensure they feel included and receive something special that is just for them.

See details at http://www.letterboxclub.org.uk/

Section 6: Looking to the Future

Just as society is not static, so the ideas that concern and surround it need to evolve, change and come from a variety of sources too. As we move forward some of the terminology and the ideas in this publication are likely to date. It feels appropriate to lend voice to some of the authors, established and new, who are challenging some of the stereotypes and narrow demographic perspectives that have long been the preserve of children's literature, offering them the chance to give ideas as to why diversity is important, what it means to them and how they feel school libraries can help in furthering this important agenda.

I therefore asked a range of friends and colleagues to outline and explain the following:

1 To outline a little about their background

2 To explain why diversity matters to them

3 To detail a strategy/activity that could be used by schools librarians.

This is a simple exercise that could be replicated with students, teachers, parents and stakeholders of your school to gain an deeper understanding of what your colleagues and others associated with the school feel are priorities and, in so doing, to help you to determine a direction of travel.

Here are the answers that I received…

Anne Fine

Author, first novelist to be honoured as UK Children's Laureate[17]

Background

I've been a reader since I was four years old, and practically lived in libraries as a child. In my twenties I started writing for children and I've carried on ever since. Unlike many writers, I've always refused to review because being able to read what I want, when I want, and without having to have some journalistic or academic response to it at the back of my mind has always been crucial to me. I'm your classic 'free reader' and hard as it is to face the idea, I know that if I had to give up writing or reading, I'd give up writing.

Why Diversity Matters

Reading broadens horizons. This is a complicated and varied world, and the more we understand other people and other cultures, the wiser we become. Reading also encourages self-reflection: 'I'm not at all like that.' 'Why, that's exactly how I feel!' 'How strange it would be to have that particular experience.' So it's important that our reading reflects the widest range of possibilities. Understanding leads to tolerance and acceptance, and in a tense and crowded world we need as much of both those qualities as we can get.

---

[17] Fine, Anne, (2017), Personal Correspondence [15/03/2017]

Writers are all the better for being honest about the deepest feelings. We need these diverse voices to explain what's truly going on inside and around the lives and minds of people we might never otherwise understand.

Suggestion

Suppose schools fearlessly came way up front with the diversity issue? Suppose they asked each child to choose the way in which she or he sometimes feels most 'diverse' – be it by race or colour, religion, sexuality, being 'on the spectrum', dyslexic, having a visual or hearing impairment, or behavioural problems, or whatever. Suppose the children were each asked to share a book that illuminated the issue for them – either a book they already know, or after researching online. You might need to get the purchase of a few books sponsored. But I expect you'd end up with a far wider selection of reading.

Giancarlo Gemin (G. R. Gemin)

Author of *Cow Girl* and *Sweet Pizza*[18]

Background

I was never a child reader (or writer for that matter), in fact I struggled with English. I've always believed that hard work can overcome the lack of natural ability. I've never thought of myself as a natural writer. To be honest, the enjoyment of reading came to me in my late-twenties.

Why Diversity Matters

Growing up in an Italian immigrant family and having Erb's Palsy (that's a limited physical paralysis on one side of the body) the need for diversity, and of course inclusion, is vital. It's horrible to feel excluded or overlooked. It makes you feel worthless and isolated. Equally, and to this day, I never want a fuss made or compensations that only emphasise being different. Without diversity we encourage segregation, low self-worth and exclusion, and I believe the vast majority of people wouldn't want that.

Suggestion

The one thing I would say to libraries is not to be prescriptive about who uses a library and why. There will always be children who, like me as a child, do not read a great deal. If they think libraries are only for people with their nose in a book we are lost. Having worked in social care and schools my experience is that people of any age seldom ask or say what they want. So we have to use our imagination to engage people across the community, because when an initiative works you will know it.

---

18 Gemin, Giancarlo (2017), Personal Correspondence [09/03/2017]

Steve Tasane

Author of *Blood Donor* and *Nobody Saw No One*[19]

Background

I grew up with three brothers and my Mum on a council estate, dirt poor, as they say. I still consider working class characters – of whatever ethnic background – to be grossly underrepresented in children's fiction. I think contemporary children's publishers are – quite rightly – specifically addressing a host of 'issues' that have previously been underwritten about – whether racism, homophobia, gender issues, drugs, the plight of refugees. However, I'd like to see working class characters in books that aren't about poverty; black characters in books that aren't about race; gay characters in books that aren't about being gay – etc. We are all normal. We all share the same wonder at fabulous stories. So why should we feel excluded from mainstream storytelling? My Mum was a single mum, but my Dad was an Estonian refugee who fled his Russian-occupied homeland. So, the prejudice I experienced as a child in 1960s Yorkshire was subtle and hard to identify: On the one hand, I had an odd name – Tasane – and a strange accent; on the other, my refugee father was absent from my life; on the other hand, being brought up by a single parent was rare and shameful in those days – it was referred to as a 'broken home'. But on the third hand, as it were, I had white skin. I never experienced racism from strangers, threats and abuse on the street because of my race. I never got queerbashed. I never got my bottom pinched by workmen. I understand my relative privilege. Indeed, it took me decades before I understood that my unhappy childhood was caused by other people's prejudices towards my own differences. And it took me decades before I even began to describe myself as the child of a refugee (That felt fake. How could that be?) But I instinctively empathised with any kind of 'outsider' character in stories, and I always found myself writing from an 'outsider' point-of-view. What was Queen's English to me? I was Yorkshire/Estonian Pov!

Why Diversity Matters

Diversity is important because we are all important. No child – or adult – should feel excluded from mainstream stories. It is an integral way in which our imagination works with stories that we are able to picture ourselves within the story. So why are the majority of characters automatically white? Why are they automatically financially stable? If there is no reason within a plot for a character to be white middle class, why do so many authors insist on portraying them as white middle class? In my own books, unless the plot demands otherwise, I ensure that my characters can be read as people of colour, or gay. But they can also be read as white and straight. The point is, I refuse to make a presumption; *presumption* is the benign starting point of prejudice. The only specific distinction I make in my writing is, in general, that my characters are working class, because of my own class background; and because I always felt I wasn't allowed to join in with the Famous Five gang as a kid because my clothes were tatty and I had a *foreign* name and no dad. For me, my novel *Blood Donors* was just the Famous Five with added diversity (and killer bloodsucking bugs!)

Suggestion

Be fearless! Don't be afraid of the Zone of Discomfort! Welcome the stranger.

---

[19] Tasane, Steve, (2017), Personal Correspondence [10/03/2017]

Chris Moore

Blogger and Social Media Influencer[20]

Background

I am a book blogger and influencer who has completed numerous internships with publishing companies including Egmont Publishing and HarperCollins Publishers. I read and promote (mostly) Young Adult literature on my blog, and occasionally, some Children's and Adult Fiction. I have spent the last couple of years working with, and promoting, *The Lancashire Book of the Year Award, Manchester Children's Book Festival* and *YA Shot*. I will never stop championing diversity. There will always be voices that need to be heard and stories that need to be told. There will always be a place for the stories in our world so it's up to all of us to ensure that these stories get to the right people and that everyone feels like they belong in our world.

Why Diversity Matters

When I was ten, I lost interest in books. I extensively read R. L. Stine's *Goosebumps* for years and suddenly, I just… stopped. I loved the horror and the sheer escapism in those books but when it came to processing questions around my sexuality, I didn't need to read about characters that slept with one eye open because their psychotic dummy was going to murder them in their sleep. I needed books that dealt with the real questions I was dealing with: am I normal? Who am I and does my sexuality change this? This is not a sly dig at fantasy and horror genres because they can (and do) include diverse people and weave similar issues into their stories but I, unfortunately, chose a series that didn't portray characters that I could relate to or issues similar to mine. More than any of this, there was a black hole in my local library and bookshop for stories that dealt with LGBT issues and characters.

Eight years later, I decided to come out and after eight years of not reading anything other than newspaper headlines and core texts for English literature, it would have been very difficult for me to jump back into reading. The first book I picked up very well could have been my last. Luckily, I picked up David Levithan's *Boy Meets Boy* and while I felt it could have been pushed further in terms of the characters and the issues they dealt with, I felt a sense of belonging. I could relate to these characters. I could empathise with their fears and share in their accomplishments. I could laugh and it spoke to my subconscious and planted the first idea of 'coming out' after so many years of trying to tell myself that I was wrong and I would have to hide who I was to belong.

Gone are the days when I walked with my head held low and a shuffling gait. We all have the power to promote diversity, share multiple viewpoints and live thousands of different lives in our lifetimes. Reading different points of view gives us different lenses through which to view the world, allowing us a deeper understanding of issues, including, and not limited to, sexuality, gender, ethnicity, class, mental health and disability, increasing tolerance and acceptance of different ideas and people.

---

[20] Moore, Chris, (2017), Personal Correspondence [10/02/2017]

Suggestion

People are always looking for recommendations. I sometimes wonder what trajectory my life and career might have taken were it not for the fact I chanced upon David Levithan's book. Libraries could make use of shelf-recommendations, short precis of books by librarians, teachers and students themselves so that other readers are able to have a glimpse as to what is on offer inside the book covers.

Catherine Johnson

Author of *Nest of Vipers*, *The Curious Tale of the Lady Caraboo* and others[21]

Background

I've been a published writer for 24 years, and worked in literature development and taught in universities and local authority classes. I've mentored lots of children's writers too. My books have never been big sellers, but I have been nominated for awards and won one once(!) with *Sawbones*, for historical writing for young readers, and been an IBBY White Raven nomination, for *Landlocked*. I've been shortlisted for the YA prize with *The Curious Tale Of The Lady Caraboo*. I read very, very widely. I still do some school visits with books. My latest book is *Blade & Bone*.

Why Diversity Matters

I grew up never seeing myself in books. In fact the first time I did was in school aged 15 when we did *To Kill A Mockingbird* in which Scout goes to the black part of town with Jem, and sees mixed children, who Jem tells her are the saddest people 'because they don't fit in anywhere' and 'nobody wants them'. That was the only time I read about anyone like myself. And that was the message. Of course these days people like me are fairly well represented in all parts of culture except books. And this continues today. Why do we think white readers won't read books with other races? Well maybe we do if the writer is white, or maybe will in future when non-white writers are confident and of better quality than we are now. (Sorry that was sarcasm.)

But really why it matters is because it excludes new readers and it excludes writers of the future. The world of books, society says, is not for you.

Suggestion

It's hard because while publishers publish a small number of inclusive books, these are often not publicised or marketed. Is that because they are less worthwhile? If we take publication as a sign of quality, perhaps school libraries should look at making sure they have books that feature and are by authors from a wider range of backgrounds/gender/sexuality/disability as well as race. After all wouldn't librarians think it odd if all their books were only by men (or women?) wouldn't they make an effort to address that? Using specialist organisations like Letterbox Library as consultants would be an excellent first step.

---

[21] Johnson, Catherine, (2017), Personal Correspondence [13/03/2017]

Debi Gliori

Author and illustrator of numerous titles including *Night Shift* which offers understanding and awareness around depression[22]

Background

I was born to older, middle-class parents who'd dragged themselves out of their working-class roots by dint of reading and sheer determination to succeed. They encouraged me to read from an early age, read to me and bought lots of books to lay down a habit of reading that I still love to this day. As a child, I was very solitary and bookish, preferring to live in the imaginary world of fiction to the real world of Glasgow in the late 60s early 70s. I went to Art College mainly because I wanted to make a living in illustrating books. At that point I had no idea that I might be able to write them. I don't watch much TV if any at all, and spend at least two to three hours before bedtime, reading fiction. And always have.

Why Diversity Matters

Diversity (along with climate warming) is one of the most important issues that face our planet and its people. I don't see any difference between races and people, between abilities and disabilities; as far as I am aware, we are all one species, one tribe under the sun. The disagreements and factionalism and nationalism and tribalism in its worst sense that divide our world today are distracting us all from the most important issues of our time; namely, how to peacefully co-exist, how to spread the abundance of our planet's resources in an equal fashion and how to come together and do something to mitigate the worst effects of climate warming. We are diverse in our thoughts and abilities, obviously, diverse in what we can all bring to the table, but we are all the same in what we need; water, food, shelter, love and a safe place to live. Until we recognise that this is the same, should be the same entitlement for every living being, we will have no hope of living as one race on our planet.

Suggestion

A rotating student council who are part of the decision-making process around how the library is run, how it uses its funding and what it could and should offer to its student body. The rotation of pupils should be such that everyone has to serve on the council at some point.

Will Hill

Author of *After the Fire*, whose character Moonbeam experiences Post Traumatic Stress [23]

Background

I was lucky enough to grow up in a house full of books – my mother and stepfather were (and still are) both big readers. My mum was always happy to take me to the library, and books were the one thing my parents were always willing to buy me.

---

22 Gliori, Debi, (2017), Personal Correspondence [13/03/2017]

23 Hill, Will (2017), Personal Correspondence [17/03/2017]

Like a lot of my generation (I'm thirty-eight in 2017) I moved from children's books to adult books without the bridge that is now provided by YA. When I was a teenager and had discovered Stephen King, my mum would scout every charity shop and second-hand bookshop for anything with his name on the cover and bring them home (I suspect she was at least slightly concerned about their content, although she never said so!).

Books have been the enduring love of my life, in all honesty. I worked in a bookshop when I was at university, worked in publishing for six years after I graduated, and now I write them for a living. I read less now than I once did (I find reading and writing at the same time very difficult) but I always have at least one book on the go at any given time.

Why Diversity Matters

Firstly, because we live in a diverse world and the expectation that fiction should show that to its readers really shouldn't be too much to ask. Secondly, because everyone should have the opportunity to recognise themselves in books. I was (and still am) privileged enough to never have to look very far for a novel featuring someone who looked and sounded like me, or who came from the same background as I did. That made it easier for me to imagine that I could do the things that those characters did, that their (far more interesting and exciting) lives could be my life. That experience is valuable, and should be available to everyone.

Suggestion

I think the most valuable thing that libraries offer are knowledgeable librarians that can make recommendations based on previous books children have enjoyed, or on the kind of story a child wants to read. An extension of that might be a means of recommendations for children who might be nervous of asking for advice: it could be 'If you liked this novel, try...' stickers in the backs of books, or 'For fans of...' shelves set aside to guide readers on from the most popular books. Making the recommended selections as diverse as possible would help to introduce a broad range of topics and experiences in an organic way.

Katrina Gutierrez

Communications and Project Manager, Lantana Publishing[24]

Background

I'm the Communications & Project Manager of Lantana Publishing. We are a small, independent London-based publisher dedicated to producing diverse and inclusive books that all children can enjoy. I also have a PhD in Children's Literature from Macquarie University, Sydney.

Why Diversity Matters

I grew up not seeing myself in the books and films I read and loved. I felt that wonderful adventures only happened to girls with blonde hair and blue eyes. I am Filipino, and I got the message loud and clear that my black hair and brown skin meant that I could never be the hero – only the sidekick (with the weird accent) or the villain. What's more, most stories about Asians are

---

[24] Gutierrez, Katrina, (2017), Personal Correspondence [17/03/2017]

very stereotypical. We need diverse and inclusive books to show young readers that they are not confined to a single story or stereotype. I love working at Lantana because our book production is anchored on this central idea: 'Because *all* children deserve to see themselves in the books they read.'

Suggestion

Integrating diverse books in book displays or recommended reads that are based on themes that emphasize common humanity and life experiences, rather than separating books according to racial, cultural or other forms of difference. It would help if these books were regularly updated to show the wealth of perspectives the world has to offer.

Alex Strick

Co-founder of Inclusive Minds and Consultant[25]

Background

I grew up with a writer-father, lexicographer-mother and an innate passion for reading, so it's definitely in my blood. Career-wise, I started out working directly with children (including young disabled people) and developed a strong interest in involving and empowering young people. So when I started working at BookTrust back in the 1990s, consultation, inclusion and accessibility were already at the forefront of my thinking. Now self-employed, I continue to work as a consultant to the wonderful BookTrust but have also worked with like-minded colleagues to develop two initiatives – Outside In World (exploring and promoting books from around the world and Inclusive Minds (a collective for all those who want to see greater inclusion and diversity in books).

Why Diversity Matters

To me ' diversity' actually means 'everyone'. So it's about including ALL of us. That is why I am flabbergasted when anyone describes books or projects relevant to this field as 'niche'! I also think there can sometimes be a risk that 'diversity' is used as a shorthand to mean culture/ethnicity when actually it encompasses so many facets – gender, family structure, sexual orientation, disability, class… the list is almost endless. For that reason, at Inclusive Minds we tend to talk more about the importance of 'including everyone', as opposed to 'improving diversity'.

Suggestion

At the risk of appearing to plug Inclusive Minds again, I would urge everyone to sign up to the 'Everybody In' charter which is a simple (and free) way of pledging your commitment to this area whilst also highlighting several specific actions you plan to take in order to improve inclusivity in your specific area of work – http://www.everybodyin.co.uk/

---

25 Strick, Alex, (2017), Personal Correspondence [17/03/2017]

Pamela Berry

Vlogger, Student of Library and Information Science[26]

Background

I'm a blogger, aspiring author and Library student (currently studying). As a life-long avid reader, I've always enjoyed the transformative power of literature, and the way that a good story can take you on adventures beyond the realms of everyday life, or offer insights into experiences miles apart from your own, be it through race, gender, sexuality or historical period.

Why Diversity Matters

As a person with a disability (from birth) I was always disappointed in how, whenever I came across a character with a disability, whether visible or invisible, they were always a side-line character, or treated as the other; un-welcomed, or unlovable., an irritation to the protagonist, and never ever the hero. I knew there were reasons for this of course, such as the author not knowing any different, or at least that's how I justified it to myself as a child.

As an adult, and as somebody with library experience, I've seen first-hand the difference it can make to a child's life, when they come across a book where the main character, the hero, is more like them, in appearance or lifestyle, or by the trials that they go through and overcome through the journey within the confines of the story. The right book can do a lot of good for the self-esteem of the reader, it can lead to a boost in confidence, self-acceptance, provide tools for explaining difficult subjects or complex emotions to others.

Suggestion

Themed promotions would be a good starting point, tying displays into recent events or trends, e.g. black history month, PRIDE, shelf-help, bullying, etc. Make it easier for the right book to reach the reader.

Andrew Beasley

Author of *S.C.R.E.A.M. The Mummy's Revenge*[27]

Background

My first words, according to my mum, were 'read a book' and that is pretty much what I've been doing ever since. I read law at University. I read to my class now that I'm a teacher. I read every day to my own children. Oh, and I write books too. Just for the record, my son's first words were 'where's the matches' but that's another story.

Why Diversity Matters

We're all the same but different, okay. It really is as simple and as profound as that.

---

[26] Berry, Pamela, (2017), Personal Correspondence [15/03/2017]

[27] Beasley, Andrew, (2017), Personal Correspondence [13/03/2017]

I spent nearly two years of my life with a paralyzed arm – having done myself some serious damage whilst singing the Mission Impossible theme tune (sad but true).

That experience gave me real insight into quite how different my life could be.

I was still me in every sense that mattered; same hopes and aspirations; same friends and family; same sense of humour. What had changed was that I could no longer cut up my own food or even dress myself without help.

As a writer, naturally, I wrote about my experience. Slowly. Using just the one hand. The book remains unpublished. 'We do not publish humour,' replied one publisher, 'and if we did, we would not publish you.' Thanks for that.

Now, with the full use of my left arm fully regained (with the addition of some massive scars which I can attribute to 'shark attack') the experience of being 'disabled' remains a vivid one.

Walk for a mile in my shoes, someone wiser than me once said. I would add to that, try not using one arm for a day. Like I said, we're the same you and I. But different.

Suggestion

First of all I have to say that school libraries already do an amazing job. I know a lot of school librarians and I take my hat off to them. That's not a metaphor, I do have an actual hat.

One idea to change school libraries? Fling wide the doors.

Libraries could, and should, have all the classic titles that children (and parents) expect, but that can end up like giving kids the same thing for tea every night – you know they're going to eat it, but wouldn't it be wonderful if they tried something new for a change?!

Like most teachers, I work in a multicultural school. Every year I co-ordinate our celebration of global diversity in which parents are invited to come in and share whatever they want about their country. On that day our school throngs with exotic national dress and the aromas of a hundred new foods for the children to try. In the library, in quiet corners, in classes, the children sit and listen to stories from around the world. The same, but different, tales which bring us all together.

So fling wide those library doors, I say! Let's hear stories that are so precious that people hand them down from generation to generation and count them amongst their most precious possessions when life uproots them from one land and plants them in another.

Alex Wheatle

Author of *Liccle Bit* and *Crongton Knights*[28]

Background

I grew up in a brutal care home and in my early years, as a form of escapism, I would immerse myself in comics and football/sports annuals. That is my earliest memory of reading. My formal reading included the Peter & Jane books.

Why Diversity Matters

Diversity is important to me because I believe every child/student at school should be able to relate to a character in a book. This helps foster a belief that they are a part of society and that they can also contribute to society. Of course we all have different opinions of books but I believe librarians should be aware that narratives that reflect the lives of minority readers can have a great impact on the reader... If I may give you an example. One of my favourite reggae albums is *The Right Time* by the Mighty Diamonds. Perhaps many people have never heard of this album but for me, living as a young black male in Brixton in the late 1970s and early 1980s, the album spoke directly to me about my cultural history, my place in society, my identity, the pride of my Jamaican ancestors and the struggle that had taken place for me to be here. It's a very personal choice. Reading can have the same impact on those who may feel marginalised. If others do not value my choice who haven't lived my experiences, it doesn't lessen the impact of that album to me and its importance to me. So I think librarians, who may have their own very personal choices in what books shaped them and had an impact on them, should be aware of the life-changing potential a novel with diverse characters can have on a BAME student and value that potential.

Suggestion

My one idea? That's a tough one. Perhaps a recommendation scheme where students who have enjoyed books can recommend them to others in a monthly librarian blog. I think this is a good way of promoting books in schools.

Patrice Lawrence

Author of *Orangeboy*[29]

Background

I had early exposure to books by everyone around me. I was privately fostered until I was four and my foster mum, Aunty Phylis, joined me up to the local library and taught me to read. My mum is also a voracious reader and she was very much into the classics. What was good, though, was she would read them first and then encourage me to read them so we could talk about them. *The Wind in the Willows, Alice in Wonderland, the Water Babies, Heidi, The Secret*

---

[28] Wheatle, Alex, (2017), Personal Correspondence [14/03/2017]

[29] Lawrence, Patrice, (2017), Personal Correspondence [12/03/2017]

Garden, The Jungle Book, Anne of Green Gables, Little Women – though *Children of the New Forest* and *Lorna Doone* defeated me. School libraries introduced me to Swallows, Amazons and Wishing Chairs. Friends handed me C. S. Lewis and Famous Fives. The first YA seeds were sown without me noticing when Mr Jones, my English teacher in what's now Year 8, made us read Paul Zindel's *The Pig Man*. People seriously wrote books like that? About real teenagers? So, over to Haywards Heath library, devouring all the Zindels followed by the SE Hintons.

And in the hundreds and hundreds of books I read before I was sixteen, there was never a character that could have been me. In my mid-teens, when I felt isolated, ugly and unwanted, I can only imagine the difference it would have made to read a book with a young black British heroine who came near to how I felt. Instead, I ended up watching 'Single White Female' wondering if I was the only one thinking that the major premise was flawed. ('Single White Female seeks same...')

Why Diversity Matters

In my 30s, while studying an MA in writing For Film and TV, I discovered the book *Black Looks* by author bell hooks. Suddenly, the world made sense. All my life, I had to undertake an identity cleanse when watching films and reading books. Someone who looked like me would never be the romantic, the lead or the plucky heroine that saved the day. It's a drip drip message that infiltrates your everyday life – you are simply not good enough. I never wrote black characters because nobody would ever read them. We were not worthy of being represented. Then, in the closing weeks of 1999, while working out what I was supposed to be doing with my newborn daughter, the BBC adaptation of Malorie Blackman's *Pig Heart Boy* came on. (What *is* it about pigs?) A black British family? Telling a heartrending brilliant story – that wasn't about being black? Blimey! It wasn't just the post-birth hormones that made me burst into tears.

And Cbeebies! Loads of adults, families and children that could be us! And Helen Oxenbury's board books. And Trish Cooke's and Helen Oxenbury's *'So Much'*! It took a while to realise that that was as good as it was going to get. We peaked way too early.

We are doing young people a serious disservice by not providing a wide range of books told from a wide range of experiences. Young people are better than that. They are empathetic, curious and open-minded. In Newcastle, white young men and women who'd shortlisted *Orangeboy* for the North East Teen Book Awards, told me how much they enjoyed it. The main character may be a 16-year-old black boy in London, but they totally 'got' the themes about agency, authority, family pressure. Lisa Williamson won with *'The Art of Being Normal'*. She said that some young people had told her that this was the only LGBT book in their school library – they were now campaigning for more.

Suggestion

Activities are empty and unsustainable if the people doing them are ambivalent. I'd suggest an initial facilitated session with someone like Letterbox Library or Mark Jennett to unlock the issues and concerns. (In another life, I invited Mark to deliver a workshop about LGBT children's books to a conference of early years workers who have a tendency to be somewhat conservative. They loved him.) Once librarians understand why it matters, they will be putting books in hands. Monitor stock and take up. Develop a vision about the role of the library and the books within it – escape, empathy, education, stimulating curiosity, understanding the world around them. Make an action plan. Set dates to update and monitor it.

When I was about nine, before the advent of video-players, schools had to rely on the BBC schools programmes. You'd have a date with the TV room at a certain time and the TV would be wheeled in on a trolley-thing. I remember sitting there, the only black kid in the class. The programme that came on was about the Caribbean – about Anansi stories and paime, a Trinidad treat made from cornmeal, coconut and pumpkin, often cooked in banana leaves. I remember realising that I had a heritage that mattered and how happy my mum was when I told her about the programme. In a sense, it validated her memories; we didn't have to hide who we are. It also showed the children around me that other people have special stories, special meals.

Librarians can help children have those moments from the day they start school.

Ifeoma Onyefulu

Author and photographer of books including *A is for Africa* and *Deron goes to Nursery School*[30]

Background

I worked as a freelance photographer for Black newspapers before I became a children's author.

I have written 23 books for children, and have won a few awards in America, one of which was CABA (Children Africana Book Award) twice for *Here Comes Our Bride* and for *Ikenna Goes to Nigeria*. Also, my first book *A is for Africa*, was nominated for the CILIP Kate Greenaway Medal.

I am often invited to libraries, and to schools in the UK, America, Hong Kong, Nigeria and others to do workshops.

Why Diversity Matters

Diversity is important indeed, and must be encouraged, especially now that we have Brexit, and because more and more people are becoming very insular and there is the fear of foreigners. How do we break down those walls?

We must remember that a lot connects us all, and also we must celebrate our differences too. Diversity also helps us to learn about the world around us, especially for our children, who are the future generation.

Suggestion

Encourage children to explore the many cultures around us and in books, and to raise the advantages of learning from others, which enriches one's culture and breaks down fears of the other. It brings everyone a lot closer, too.

---

[30] Onyefulu, Ifeoma (2017), Personal Correspondence [22/03/2017]

Cordelia Fine

Academic and author of *Delusions of Gender* and '*Testosterone Rex: Unmaking the Myths of our Gendered Minds*'[31]

About You

I'm a professor of History & Philosophy of Science at the University of Melbourne with a background in psychology, and also a writer. So I spend a lot of my work life reading, as well as thinking about what to get my students to read that will best get them to think, get them interested in a topic, and question their assumptions. In one of the areas I teach – ethical leadership – there's growing interest in using fiction to get students to self-reflect, consider other perspectives, recognize what they have in common with people who at first seem quite different, and better understand human psychology. I also read as much as I can for pleasure.

Why Diversity Matters

For me, there are two main reasons that diversity is important. Pragmatically, we know there are benefits of 'cognitive heterogeneity' – having teams made up of people with different training, expertise and experiences – for problem-solving, innovation and decision-making. The second reason is the importance, ethically, for decision-making power to be distributed in a way that reflects the values, interests and concerns of the entire community, not a relatively homogeneous subset of it. For both reasons, the sooner people find others not 'like me' better humanized through their reading, and expand their view of whose voices and experiences count and deserve attention, the better.

Suggestion

One of the mantras of the business world is that organizations only change what they measure. Whose voices and experiences are represented in books, events and activities? We're so used to hearing certain kinds of stories, that it's easy to overestimate how much diversity there really is in media.

Glenda Millard

Author of *The Stars at Oktober Bend*[32]

Background

I grew up on the outskirts of a small rural town in Victoria, Australia. My father was a labourer at a factory. I left school at fifteen and began work as a junior clerk.

One of my earliest and fondest memories is of my sister and I lying one either side of mum in bed while she read to us from a book of fairy tales. What better way to grow a child's imagination? What better way to establish a love of reading, than to be read to in the arms of a person who loves you?

---

31 Fine, Cordelia, (2017), Personal Correspondence [21/03/2017]

32 Millard, Glenda, (2017), Personal Correspondence [24/03/2017]

We didn't own a television until I was about 18. My parents were both keen readers, but there wasn't a lot of money to spare and books were precious gifts, given on birthdays and at Christmas. I treasured Enid Blyton's books along with *Black Beauty, Little Women* and *Anne of Green Gables*. Apart from these and books I borrowed from the school library, I read whatever I could find at home. An eclectic mix by any standards; poetry by the likes of Henry Lawson and Banjo Patterson, paperback 'Westerns' and 'Big Game' hunting stories, Georgette Heyer novels and second-hand comics passed on by our cousins.

At high school I used to write stories, hoping to be published in the annual school magazine, the aim being to win a prize – usually a voucher at the bookstore in town.

I never had any tertiary education but books taught me what I needed to know and still do.

Why Diversity Matters

Diversity enriches us, enables us to empathise and reassures us that it's okay to be us.

Suggestion

Purchase books which positively reflect diversity for your library. Read and review them on a blog for students.

Amy McKay

School Librarian, Corby Business Academy, SLA School Librarian of the Year 2016[33]

Background

I've been a school librarian in Northamptonshire for the last 12 years and truly believe I have the best job in the world. Every day is different and I've been lucky to work with some amazing people – both staff and students in school, and other librarians and bookish people outside school. I'm an avid reader myself and am rarely without a book. I was named SLA School Librarian of the Year 2016 and am the National Coordinator of the Carnegie and Kate Greenaway Medals. I was enrolled as a member of my local public library at 6 months old and have never looked back.

Why Diversity Matters

Books and reading have the power to change the world and open up the world, everybody deserves the opportunity to benefit from this opportunity.

It's important to me that my library serves all students in the school, not just traditional library users and readers, a big part of this is ensuring we have a wide range of books that reflect and appeal to all our students.

I was the grand old age of 35 before I read a book that fully encapsulated my experiences as a mixed-raced teen and reading that book was an important moment for me. 35 years as a reader and 11 years working directly with books, and I was shocked and delighted to discover my own experiences reflected. I read passages from the book to anybody who'd listen and can quote

---

33 McKay, Amy, (2017), Personal Correspondence [03/04/2017]

many of them by heart. If only I'd had access to a book like that as a teen, maybe it would have taken a lot less time for me to better understand and feel comfortable with my place in the world. We owe all young people the life-affirming experience the opportunity to see themselves in books offers.

Those of us who work with and love books often cite empathy building as one of the many benefits of reading, especially for young people. Empathy though will only grow in the reader if they are exposed to a diverse range of books and characters. We owe young people the chance to experience lives other than their own, the chance to understand people who (in whatever way) are different to themselves. For example, students in my school who have read *The Art of Being Normal* have been much more accepting and better at supporting transgender students as a result. Diverse books have the power to make the world a better place for everybody.

Suggestion

Displays – we have made a commitment in my library that at least one of our 4 display boards will always be used to promote diverse books – recent displays include #Black Lives Matter, The Most Important F Word and PRIDE. These displays draw attention to books that deal with diversity and result in an uptake in students reading them. They also establish the fact that the library is a welcoming, diversity friendly space to anybody who comes in – students have told us that these displays help normalise their experiences and, at a time when they feel they need to be just like everybody else, celebrate individual differences.

We produce booklists on many, many topics (including LGBT, books by and/or about POC, books about disabilities, books about mental health etc.) that students can access both in the library and online. This allows those students who don't feel confident enough to ask for recommendations to still access them.

We're aware that for some students who are dealing with sensitive issues even bringing books to the desk to have issued can be off putting. To combat this we've put small notes on the inside cover of certain books explaining that if the student doesn't feel able to have the book issued they're allowed to take it anyway and return it when they're ready. Book losses have been minimal and I figure I'd rather have a lost book and have helped a student, than keep the book and not have it reach those who most need it.

We ensure that books we use for specific activities promote diversity. For instance, we recently held a book quiz for 5 local schools and asked teams of students to read 20 books beforehand. These 20 books included a diverse range of issues and styles. Likewise, a poetry recital challenge I'm running at the moment uses 20 diverse texts.

Malorie Blackman

Author and Former Children's Laureate[34]

Background

My name is Malorie Blackman and I've been an author for 27 years. It was my love of reading that lead to my desire to be an author. I've written over sixty books for all ages. I was also the eighth UK Children's Laureate.

Why Diversity Matters

To be honest, I'm disappointed that in the 21st century this is still a question and an issue. True diversity is not merely important but vital to ensure that everyone is respected and regarded equally. Diversity in our children's books in particular shows all our children that we all belong, that we all make up the world in which we live and that all of our stories are valid. Diversity in this context surely equates to inclusion. It ensures that all our children inherently know and believe that they are part of the society they inhabit and that society is something in which they have a stake because their stories are equally valid and their voices heard.

Suggestion

Non-fiction books should include the stories of pioneers, scientists, inventors, achievers from around the world. These should include the lives of those from different races, genders, sexual orientations, classes, physical challenges, etc. Fiction stories should also be drawn from a wide range of authors and illustrators, as with non-fiction. This is incredibly important for *all* our children, including in schools where the racial mix may not be as great as in other parts of the country. All of our children need to be shown that it is possible and desirable to read about, experience and empathise with the lives of others who are different to ourselves.

---

[34] Blackman, Malorie, (2017), Personal Correspondence [21/03/2017]

Also available from the SLA

Supporting Autistic Students in the School Library: A Personal Perspective

by Karen Bainbridge

978-1-911222-13-2   £7.50 (SLA members £5.00)

VOICES

School librarians work across the school with all and everyone – interacting in a professional manner with busy and sometimes stressed staff and students, both in and out of lessons. An effective social manner, good behaviour techniques and a calm, caring and listening attitude all go a long way to solving problems, answering enquiries, finding that special book or resource that the user needs at that time, or perhaps by providing a haven of peace and calm for study or contemplation. Here Karen Bainbridge, an experienced school librarian, explains how she helps her students on the autism spectrum (ASD). Communication and social interaction are both challenges for these sometimes confused and anxious students and the author explains her understanding, techniques, patience and usually her success at dealing with these users. This publication will demonstrate the guidance and patience needed to bring the best out of this vulnerable but valuable group of users that can help to turn the library into a haven for them and give them a lifelong interest in libraries.

New Beginnings: A Practical Guide to Taking Charge of a Secondary School Library

by Laura Taylor

978-1-911222-10-1   £13.50 (SLA members £9.00)

Taking charge of a secondary school library should be a pleasure, but can be a challenge to those who are unprepared. Here, experienced practitioner, trainer and consultant, Laura Taylor, who has worked in school libraries here and abroad, takes us through the process of taking ownership of your new library and post. She holds your hand from the first day and first week. Full of excellent advice and common sense, Laura guides you skilfully past the pitfalls, tells both fresh beginners and new appointees the questions to ask, the strategies to adopt and the planning to do to bring success both to you and to your school library.

Train to Gain: Continuing Professional Development for School Librarians

by Barbara Band

978-1-911222-09-5   £10.00 (SLA members £7.00)

Continuing Professional Development (CPD) is an important element of the career progression for all of us. Here, experienced school library practitioner, independent trainer and latterly President of CILIP, Barbara Band, reflects on the nature and range of CPD and why it is necessary. She examines the personal and organisational benefits, important aspects and possible challenges and barriers, and suggests some ways to undertake CPD in differing circumstances. This is a 'must read' publication for everyone working in school libraries who wishes to maintain their learning and keep their library knowledge credible and up to date.